RAUT

Teacher, Leader, Engineer

RAUT

Teacher, Leader, Engineer

Remembering

ROLAND RAUTENSTRAUS, P.E.
The Twelfth President of the University of Colorado

Richard Weingardt, P.E.

Published by
College of Engineering and Applied Science
University of Colorado at Boulder

Distributed by
Jacqueline Enterprises, Inc.
Denver, CO

RAUT: Teacher, Leader, Engineer by Richard Weingardt

Copyright © 1999 by Richard George Weingardt

Library of Congress Cataloging in Publication Data
Weingardt, Richard G.
RAUT: Teacher, Leader, Engineer.
Remembering Roland Rautenstraus,
The Twelfth President of the University of Colorado.
Includes bibliographical references and index.
1. Education. 2. Engineering. 3. Leadership.
4. Politics. 5. Athletics. 6. History. 7. Society.
8. Community. 9. Schools. 10. Title.

Library of Congress Catalog Card No. 99-74459

ISBN 0-932446-08-6

Printed in the United States of America

10 9 8 7 6 5 4 3 2 1

FOREWORD

By Sen. Robert Dole,
former president of the U.S. Senate

When we were growing up in Russell, Kansas, in the mid-30s, Rautie (as we called him) and I had no way of knowing our friendship would endure for a lifetime, nor could we have predicted how the world would unfold for either of us.

Though our interests diverged—his into engineering, education, and on to the presidency of one of the country's highest institutes of learning, and mine into law, politics, and eventually the U.S. Senate—our paths crossed often. Some meetings were personal, while others addressed work-related issues requiring each of our professional opinions.

As early as high school, Rautie exhibited the very characteristics that would distinguish him later in life as an orator of first rank, namely his ability to express his thoughts in an eloquent and graceful manner. He brought his respect for honor, duty, and commitment to the University of Colorado. He maintained those attributes throughout his career, both as a teacher in his early (and later-in-life) years and as the University's president in the late 1970s.

His influence did not rest at the state level in Colorado, though his successful maneuvering with legislators brought the University much needed funding. National issues of the time required him to be sensitive to life's changing social atmosphere. Even-tempered and compassionate, he dealt with the ever-revolving social climate of the day's events—Vietnam, student unrest on campuses—just as we were dealing with them in Washington.

Throughout his career, Raut (as he was known on campus) focused his concerns on teaching young people and preparing them for life. He was a student's teacher and they loved him. This rapport, along with his gregarious and generous personality, brought him respect from both students and faculty throughout his career.

His years overseeing the institution as its president helped the University acquire international stature. Doing this required many personal sacrifices on Raut's part during his career. His total commitment, devotion and loyalty to his alma mater, though, was second only to his love of teaching and his students.

He truly was a leader of the highest regard. His leadership made an impact not only at the state level, but on national and international platforms as well.

In his later years, he was an international consultant and advisor for businesses in developing countries. A recognized leader in this field, he gave lectures worldwide on how to feed and industrialize Third World countries through technology transfer. Because of his ability to see the big picture, his contributions to education and the profession of engineering were significant and visionary. A credit to Colorado and the University, Raut enhanced the national reputation of both.

He was certainly an example of a person in the right profession. He made his students want to be better than they thought they could be. He could bring out the best in a person, and he used this skill to the utmost degree as a teacher of young men and women. He taught his classes in a style that captivated students; his charisma held students in rapt attention even as he discussed the more mundane aspects of the engineering field.

When students signed up for one of Raut's courses, they learned the tenets of engineering to be sure. But they also left the class a semester later having realized something more about themselves and the world around them. Raut was like that. He always gave more than what people came for. His thoughtful, warm manner and genuine interest in his students and those around him influenced many an engineering career.

Raut lived the life he was meant to live. He was a true citizen of the world. From his beginnings in rural Kansas to the limelight of a major presidency, his personal and professional journeys inspired all who knew him. His life philosophies and professional achievements are truly accomplishments to which many may aspire. The story of how he lived illustrates how just one person can make a difference. He made the world a better place to live and I was privileged to know him.

ACKNOWLEDGMENTS

This book could not have been completed without the input, and able assistance and participation of Professor Stein Sture and Carol Rowe of the College of Engineering, University of Colorado at Boulder. They assisted, not only in the gathering of information and photographs, but also with several of the interviews. Both Stein and Carol reviewed much of the manuscript during its development, offering sage and helpful advice on the wording of certain facts.

Professor Sture is a virtual walking encyclopedia of knowledge not only about the College, but about Rautenstraus and the University itself. He was instrumental in assembling the core list—including telephone numbers and addresses—of people to interview. He also allowed the author free access to his collection of Rautenstraus speeches, a few of which are reprinted in Appendix B.

This project was dependent on the support and approval of Dean Ross Corotis and the College of Engineering, as well as that of Paul Bauman and the University of Colorado Foundation. I extend my sincere appreciation to them and their staffs. I am, likewise, thankful for the assistance provided by those at the Norlin Library Archives, and the CU* Heritage and Alumni Centers.

My sincerest appreciation goes to U.S. Senator Bob Dole for writing the Foreword and sharing his personal thoughts about his boyhood friend whom this book is about. I also extend my thanks to his fine assistant Doug MacKinnon for all his help.

The following people provided considerable assistance, including free access to personal records, photographs and documents during the research and writing on this book, and I am much indebted to them: Curt Rautenstraus, Willie Rautenstraus and Kent Rautenstraus.Several notables from the media reviewed the final draft of *RAUT*: Charles Hemming, editor of the *ASCE* News*, Lawrence Paddock, editor emeritus of the *Daily Camera* and Pam Penfold, editor of the *Coloradan*. Special thanks are extended to them and to William (Bud) Davis, author of *Glory Colorado!*, for their fine reviews and opinions about the book. Abstracts of their comments are on the back cover.

I was extremely pleased with the quality efforts of all those who reviewed the final manuscript, offered suggestions and provided editing—all of which added to making the book better. In addition to the members of the media mentioned above, those reviewers included: Curt Rautenstraus, Carol Rowe, Stein Sture, Jill Tietjen, David and Evelyn Weingardt.

I would like to acknowledge and thank the following for their contributions and outstanding work: David Weingardt for designing the book's cover, Barbara McNichol for copy-editing, Michele Ashmore for doing the final proof-

---

*Acronyms used throughout this publication are listed at the back of the book.

CU = University of Colorado; ASCE = American Society of Civil Engineers

ing and compiling the Index. The photograph used for the cover is courtesy of the *Daily Camera*.

This book is about remembering a great man and it could not have been done without the input of all those who gave freely of their time to be interviewed. There is not enough space available here to name them all but they are listed in the Sources section at the end of the book. Everyone who was interviewed had extremely interesting information and valuable data. Among the more in-depth and enlightening discussions were those with the Rautenstrauses, Larry Dumler (Raut's oldest nephew), Stan and Bob Adelstein, John Buechner, James Corbridge, Paul Danish, David Grimm, Sandy Hale and Ted Manning.

Finally, I wish to express my gratitude to my family, especially my wife, Evie, for their constant support and encouragement while I was researching and writing *RAUT*. President Rautenstraus made a tremendous impact on everyone he came into contact with, including me, and it was truly an honor and a labor of love to author this story of his life.

TABLE OF CONTENTS

1

THE RIGHT MAN
(Introduction)

His was a most successful term as president (some say one of *the* most successful in the school's history). He was at the helm when the University of Colorado celebrated its centennial, and started its move toward becoming one of America's great places of higher learning.

Charismatic and eloquent, his was a most enchanting and captivating presence. And that voice. Once you heard him speak, people would never forget the magnificent sound of his voice—low, modulated and mesmerizing. Some called him the American version of Britain's Alistair Cooke.

He was completely at ease with the highest levels of leadership: CEOs of major corporations, captains of every industry, the top educators from coast to coast, state and federal officials, governors, U.S. presidents and senators, and high foreign diplomats. He mingled with them, hosted them and was entertained by them. He created rapport with sports heroes, movie stars and entertainers. He influenced major decisions not only at the university level but in the broader community—locally, statewide, nationally and internationally.

Yet, suddenly, after just five years as president of the University when he was only 55 years old, Roland Rautenstraus—the first and only engineer to ever hold this lofty position—stepped down.

Of all the countless options and opportunities open to him, he decided to go back to teaching. Why? What would cause someone to give up all the trappings of power, prestige and fanfare to become, once again, simply a teaching professor, especially at his age?

What sort of person would do this? Specifically, who was this man so many affectionately called Raut?* What were the events—and who were the people—that affected him? And who were some of the men and women whose lives he helped mold and point in the right direction?

Roland Rautenstraus grew up in small-town, rural America, the son of a Lutheran minister, a stern German disciplinarian who had difficulty showing the softer side of his emotions. The youngest, by 10 years, of four siblings— two brothers and a sister—Roland received a lot of doting attention from them. A precocious child, he often roamed the open fields near his home, enjoying a Tom Sawyer-type life. He was raised in rugged, frontier towns with dirt roads—first in Nebraska, then Kansas—where everybody knew everyone and knew everyone's business, too.

Because his father—a minister in a God-fearing, moral and religious part of the country—was one of the most visible and respected men in town, young Roland must have been singled out and watched closely. He had just started the first grade, early at age five, when Black Thursday (October 24, 1929) hit, and the stock market crashed. His father, like everyone else, lost what money he had. Young Raut never

---

*In addition to the nickname 'Raut,' certain close friends and relatives called Rautenstraus 'Rolie.' Some spelled it 'Rollie' or Rolly.' In the text of this biography, Rolie is used.

related to his family being poor because those around him— all his friends and their families—were in the same boat.

Even though it was the Depression and his parents were inherently strict, he remembered his early school age years as being "fun and happy days." According to Rautenstraus, being the youngest in a caring family offered a lot of advantages: "There were always a lot of adults around who paid attention to me and taught me things." On a continual basis, he conversed with people older than himself, fraternized with them, played adult card games, learned to read young and, as a result, grew up early.

Once in high school, he experienced the adoration and rewards of fame outside his family and its immediate circle. He excelled both on the football field and in the classroom—a top student in most subjects, especially in speech and debate.

His first three years of high school were spent in Russell, Kansas, where he became a champion high school debater. He was a member of the Kansas Class A state championship team for both 1939 and 1940—his sophomore and junior years. The Rautenstrauses moved to Colorado between Roland's junior and senior years and, in the winter of 1940-41, he was named All-Conference in football—a 5'-11", 180-pound guard—while a senior at Wheat Ridge High School.

Young Rautenstraus and his best pals at Russell High—a Kansas county judge's son Phil Ruppenthal and Bob Dole, the future U.S. senator—would remain close after he left Kansas and for the rest of his life.

Roland did not go to college right after high school. Instead, he tried to enroll in the Navy's officers' training program but was turned down, mainly because he was only 17. He then enrolled briefly at the University of Denver but dropped out after a couple of weeks. Shortly thereafter he left home in search of a job in Las Vegas, Nevada, which is where he was on December 7, 1941, when the Japanese bombed Pearl Harbor and instantaneously brought the United States into World War II.

The Japanese action inspired countless patriotic young Americans to immediately join the Army, Navy or other branches of the armed services. Rautenstraus re-contacted the Navy about their officers' program but he was again put on hold. Nevertheless, he decided to return to Colorado and attend Colorado State College in Greeley (now the University of Northern Colorado—UNC) on a football scholarship in the fall of 1942.

After his first year at UNC, he was finally notified by the Navy of his acceptance in their V-12 officers' training program at the University of Colorado in Boulder. That meant switching from UNC and from a major in arts and science to engineering. The Navy needed engineers and was training them in Boulder. Rautenstraus accepted their challenge.

From 1943 to 1945, Roland was enrolled at CU taking an extra heavy course load to try to complete his bachelor of science degree in civil engineering in just two years. During that same period, he found time to letter in football and earn his Naval officer's commission. The latter accomplished, he was sent to the Pacific in the fall of 1945, a few credits short of his degree. He was assigned to the island of Okinawa near newly conquered Japan where the Navy's Seabees were building runways and other construction projects. There, he rose to the rank of lieutenant. While in the service, he picked up two (nearly) life-long obsessions— the fear of flying and smoking.

Upon his return to Boulder in the spring of 1946, the University hired him as an engineering instructor even though he had not yet finished his degree course work.

On June 30, 1946, he was married—by his father Reverend Christian Rautenstraus—to his college sweetheart Willie Atler. On a beautiful, warm, cloudless day with the snowcapped Rocky Mountains as a backdrop, Roland promised her, "I'm going to take you all around the world." (That's what engineers did—they worked all around the globe.) She reported he never fulfilled that promise. They spent his entire career in Boulder at the University of Colorado.

Rautenstraus quickly progressed from the rank of instructor to professor and, at age 35, was elected by his peers to chair the College of Engineering's civil engineering department. In 1964, at age 40, he began his advance into broader-picture positions at the University, becoming the Associate Dean of Faculties. By 1974, he became the University's first executive vice president. He thus became well entrenched in the school's upper echelon of leadership.

Less than a year later, he was named the 12th president of the institution, replacing his previous boss who had been dismissed. At 51, Raut was one of CU's youngest presidents ever—a feat he accomplished without a Ph.D., the customary degree required for such a position. His appointment as head man was trumpeted by the regents, and widely accepted by CU's alumni and the public. Virtually all (including CU's current president, John Buechner) proclaimed him, "the right man at the right time for the job."

The University had been going through some turbulent times for several years and the Board of Regents felt Rautenstraus was the man who could change that. Its members were sure that his special, open and trusting style would inspire people to work together for the common good and a higher purpose. Regent Jack Anderson said, "When we fired Raut's predecessor, we were hopeful Raut would bring calm to a chaotic situation. And he did."

He brought something more to the presidency. "The major distinguishing characteristic of Raut from the presidents who preceded him and followed him was his genuine love for the students—his recognition that the University existed for them—and his tremendous loyalty to and love for the University," stressed Regent Richard J. Bernick.

"He could make a person look at things differently," recalled Stan and Bob Adelstein, students of Roland's in the early 1950s and business associates from 1969 until his final days. "He was so articulate, his verbal skills were just incredible. He had the magic ability to paint a picture with words—almost like music that you don't forget. Somehow, he was able to reach into the subconscious and plant ideas in such a positive way, you could always hear—and visualize—them."

Roland was often called upon to deliver commencement addresses because he was a much-in-demand speaker. He would frequently say, "Don't live in the gray monotone world of attempting to make no errors. If you do, you will end your lives wondering if you ever lived at all, and that would be the greatest of all mistakes."

David Grimm, Roland's special assistant during his presidency, said, "Raut, with that fantastic and unique style of his, was an orator of the highest rank, right up there with the very best in the world. He made a lasting impression, not unlike a John F. Kennedy or Winston Churchill. And he had a mind like a computer for filing away facts. You couldn't bring up a subject he couldn't discuss in detail with insight and depth."

Journalist Edward Murray, who interviewed Raut halfway through his presidency, concurred, "One of the joys of interviewing Rautenstraus is that he sounds as if he just finished a day's research on whatever subject comes up. He doesn't lecture or spout facts; he targets in with the concise information most pertinent to the question." In his piece in the *Daily Camera* (January 9, 1977), Murray stated that Roland, at age 53, "looks like a movie actor, thinks precisely, like the civil engineer he is, and talks like an ethical philosopher. It's no wonder that he is president of the state university with its 30,000 students, its 1,973 faculty members and 6,309 in supporting staff, its four campuses, and its $250 million annual budget. He exudes the competence and confidence to handle the job."

During his watch as president, the University of Colorado faced many trying times and came of age. Rautenstraus had what it took to handle them and the evolution of the University from one with a single campus having several extension divisions to one with four campuses, each with its own leadership. And, just as skillfully, he dealt with a state legislature that wanted to micro-manage institutions of higher education. In addition, he dealt with restrictive funding, student unrest, a bizarre conflict with a National Football League team's owner concerning the hiring of a football coach, and an unpleasant, difficult incident with the school's first female chancellor who was hired by the Carter Administration in the first year of her term at CU.

That he could track so many things at once amazed many people. When Del Davis (BSCE '59) became CEO of Ball Corporation, he would invite his old surveying professor—at the time a vice president at the University—to visit with Davis' colleagues in upper management. When asked how he accomplished everything he did, Raut's response was, "Didn't you ever hear of keeping more than one ball in the air at once?"

His calm and even-handed leadership moved the University through the difficulties of the early-to-late 1970s. Shortly after he had reached the zenith of his long and steady journey—from the teaching ranks to the president's house—he announced in the spring of 1979 that he was stepping down. The head man was turning his back on the school's loftiest leadership position and changing direction. This man was so dedicated to his alma mater that some said, "If you took a sample of his blood, his cells would have CU on them." Yet, he wanted something else from life.

When asked what he would do next, he told the *Sunday Camera* (Boulder, September 30, 1979), "First I will take a vacation. I haven't had one in fifteen years." He then added, "I will not be president elsewhere. I know that if I went someplace else, for the first few weeks the people would be different and very exciting. Then my tomorrows would be just like my yesterdays." He could just as appropriately have said, "I've been there, done that."

Beneath the exterior, Rautenstraus was an extremely private individual. Some, like Regent Anderson, thought that "at times, he was aloof. It was hard, sometimes, to tell if he was sincere or just putting on a front for a purpose." Anderson found this trait disconcerting at times. In describing Raut's personality, his wife Willie said, "He was a complex person, difficult to typecast. He could be very quiet and thoughtful, yet gregarious. He was compassionate but did not show emotion. I never saw him cry, ever. If anyone got too close, he put up a wall to keep them out."

"He was a man in difficult times who showed incredible grace and manners," said his former assistant Grimm. "He had a goodness at the very center of his being. Raut was one of those genuinely good people in life. They don't come along that often."

This man from the central plains of America—labeled a legend in his own time by students—had a tremendous impact on shaping not only the University but the landscape of the state itself. He helped make it what it is today. The forces that influenced the character and beliefs of this eloquent, handsome engineer—this inspirational teacher of young men and women—began long before Roland Curt Rautenstraus made his first footprint on Colorado soil.

Here is his story.

2

TO AMERICA
(1883–1940)

C hristian Rautenstraus was already a zealous, serious and hard-studying young fellow—originally with dreams to be a missionary in Africa—by the time he met, courted and proposed to comely Emma Stein in 1907. Just 19, five years younger than he, she was swept off her feet by this dashing and dapper ministry student from Wurtenburg, Germany. In their engagement photograph, he is sporting a flashy goatee, flaring mustache, and a full head of hair that would thin in a few years. She is radiant and lovely, with a Mona Lisa-type smile. He seems to be in deep thought.

His had not been an easy life up to that time. Born on November 9, 1883, Christian was only five when his father George Rautenstraus, a farmer, died. A few years later, when he was 11-and-a-half, his mother Elisabeth died leaving Christian, his two sisters Maria and Katheren and a brother Willie orphans. They were split up and sent to live with different relatives. Christian went to live with an uncle. Up to that time, his family had been living in a two-level, two-family house in Hepsasau, a village in southern Germany. Christian's family resided upstairs and his grandfather downstairs. As was common in the area, their barn was connected to the house.

When he was 87 years old, Christian described the Hepsasau countryside to his youngest grandson, Kent Rautenstraus, as "having many vineyards, cherry trees, roses and beautiful flowers. Almost everything grew there. Like Italy, it was very warm. The mountains grew wildflowers, strawberries, blueberries and raspberries by the bushels."

His uncle tended sheep and Christian's first job, when he was sent to live with him, was to feed and carry water to the herd. His schooling ended at the eighth grade. At age 14, he was confirmed in nearby Weilheim and started developing—in his words—"a desire to serve the church." After stints working for a local postal office and then a department store, he started focusing on his plans for the future. He filed an application to enter the Swiss Ministry School to become a missionary in Africa. The school turned him down.

The 20-year-old then applied to and was accepted at the seminary in Breklum, Germany. Because he lacked knowledge of the Bible and theology, he persuaded one of his good friends, a school teacher, to tutor him so he could meet the entrance requirements.

During the four years he spent at the Breklum Seminary, he learned that there were not enough German-speaking ministers in America. He did not have to hear more. Turn-of-the-century frontier America became the choice location for him to start his work for the Lord. Since he had little money, his plan was further solidified by the fact that the Lutheran Church in the U.S. would pay his expenses to make the trip, if he would sign a contract to stay for at least 10 years. He signed on the dotted line.

Even though he could speak little English at the time, Christian boldly set sail for America in 1908, after he and Emma had worked out plans to rendezvous and be married there. They would get together as soon as he finished his schooling in America and was settled in. Then, once passage was secured for her, Emma (who was born in Schlesweig Holstein, Germany on February 3, 1888) would leave her parents Jacob and Christina, her brother Ernest and sister Maria, for this high adventure to America. She would never see them or Germany again.

Immigrating through New York, Christian was greatly impressed by its size and the quantity of good food served in its restaurants. He traveled to Atchison, Kansas, where he enrolled in the Western Theological Seminary. Atchison had about 20,000 people and, according to Christian's account, "a lot of black people there." On Sunday mornings, "white people would go to the Negro church because they were such good singers."

After two years at the Kansas seminary, 27-year-old Christian Rautenstraus graduated and was ordained in Russell on October 16, 1910. This was five months to the day after he and Emma married in Gothenburg, Nebraska.

The young couple's first parish—Zion Lutheran Church—was a small country church five miles north of Gothenburg. It was the place where all four of their children were born and the family remained for 18 years. On the church grounds, next to the wood-framed church with its single steeple, were a house, a barn, a chicken coop and a small vacant school house that was occasionally used for Sunday school. Their two closest neighbors, with whom they became good friends, were the Planks and the Jobmans. Both families made their living farming, as did most of the parish's 200 members.

The parish home where the Rautenstrauses lived was almost brand new when they set up household. It had a sitting room, a kitchen, a study and three bedrooms. Their first son Herbert was born in 1911, followed by Ruth in 1912 and Walter in 1914. Roland, their third son, arrived on February 27, 1924, a "late-in-life" child, nine-and-a-half years younger than his brother Walter.

Always short of money, Rev. Rautenstraus helped paint cars to supplement their income. On Sundays, he would often deliver two sermons, one in German and the other in English. Emma (alleged by Roland, in later years, to be a very fine pianist) often played the church organ and taught Sunday school. (There are no records indicating that she was paid for doing either.)

A south-central Nebraska town in the Platte River valley, Gothenburg is surrounded by rich, irrigated farm land. The area, largely settled by German and Swedish immigrant farmers, was originally the site of a fur trading post along the Oregon Trail and a Pony Express station. In the late 1890s, the ambitious town fathers promoted a wide range of industries, including shirt, pickle, bathtub and barbed wire factories, a brickyard, a brass foundry and several flour mills. When Christian and Emma first arrived, farming and the Union Pacific railroad kept the area alive and healthy.

Situated next to the river just off Interstate I-80, Gothenburg remains today a pleasant little town with tree-lined streets and a handful of small but impressive mansions from the early 1900s. Its 1996 population was 3,232. The biggest town nearby—35 miles away—is North Platte, which was home, around the turn of the century, to Buffalo Bill Cody and his Wild West Show. Cody's entourage included a colorful collection of cowboys, old army scouts and Indians, and an amazing collection of animals.

Before long, the dependable reverend "became quite well known," reported his grandson, Kent. Parishioners often invited the family out for Sunday dinner. If world events were part of the table conversations, they would have included debate about the unthinkable sinking of the "Titanic" (1912), the opening of the Panama Canal (1913), the assassination of Archduke Ferdinand and the start of World

War I (1914), and even the antics and the death of their neighboring local frontier celebrity, Buffalo Bill (1917).

Photographs of Christian, about this time, show a lean, no-nonsense-looking man with an intense and stiff demeanor. He wore thin-rimmed glasses and combed his thinning hair straight back, flat against his head. The look might suggest a stern task master—not uncommon for newly immigrated Germans of his day, who were known for being hard workers and not wearing their emotions on their sleeve.

Around 1920, with his original 10-year commitment to the Lutheran Church fulfilled, the reverend was free to go anywhere, even back home. But Christian now felt dedicated to his parish, so he and Emma opted to stay and raise their family in Nebraska. With the end of WWI, Germany was in turmoil, struggling with its war debt. The communists controlled Russia and most European countries were experiencing devastating unemployment. Many were suffering from terrible hunger. The outlook for prosperity in America—going into the roaring twenties—looked more promising.

All three of Christian and Emma's oldest children attended elementary school in a country school house a couple of miles from their church. Their classmates were mostly farm kids, the Plank and Jobman children included. After graduating from grade school, Herbert and Ruth went on to high school in downtown Gothenburg.

In the late 1920s, when Roland was only three, Christian was transferred to St. Peter's Church in Creston in eastern Nebraska, which is where Roland's siblings graduated from high school. Even though Creston was a tiny place (about 600 residents), St. Peter's was a town church and not all of its parishioners were farmers. But that was not the only reason for the move. The main reason, given later by Christian, was that Creston was closer to Midland

Lutheran College, which Herbert and Ruth planned to attend after high school.

Orvene (Plank) Sturgeon, one of the many farm kids baptized by Rev. Rautenstraus, was only five years old when the Rautenstrauses moved from Gothenburg. Even so, Orvene said she still remembers one thing about Roland: he wasn't shy as a child. Once, the reverend's family came back to visit their old parishioners, a year or so after they had left. Orvene recalled, "We were all in church, all dressed up. Roland [who was about four-and-a-half then] came up to me, put his arms around me and hugged me. It was so sweet. He always acted older than his age." Orvene added, "A lot of people said I looked a lot like Ruth [Raut's sister] when she was young and I took that as a high compliment."

For the years prior to beginning grade school, Roland enjoyed playing in the fields and open spaces around Creston. His first few years in the small town were remembered by Raut as being completely carefree. Then things changed drastically. In September 1929, when he was five-and-a-half years old, Roland started the first grade. After he was in school only a couple of months, the stock market suddenly crashed. Rev. Rautenstraus, along with almost everyone else, lost what money he had, putting Herbert and Ruth's current plans for a college education into jeopardy.

"My father went three years without getting any salary whatsoever [as a minister]. So we were absolutely devoid of money in the family," recalled Roland. Times were bleak, indeed, but the family toughed it out together. Everyone, including all four siblings, took on any odd jobs they could find.

His brother and sister, Herbert and Ruth, Raut told a television audience in 1996*, "were adamant about going

---

*From the June 1966 TV Special, "The Depression Years," on Channel 54, Boulder, CO. Rautenstraus was the main speaker for the special program.

to college. So they struck a deal with a one-room rural school that had about 15 students. They agreed to be their teachers and they alternated years. The one who was teaching gave the full salary earned to the person who was in college to pay the bill. They did that off and on for years to finance their education." It prolonged their college days but both eventually prevailed and received their degrees. Herbert was interested in becoming a conservationist and Ruth wanted to be an elementary school teacher.

Roland often recounted how, when he got older, he helped his brothers with a small farm, doing work for local farmers, selling eggs and raising chickens—"hundreds and hundreds of chickens," he once emphasized. "I think these kinds of things—people pulling together and neighbors helping neighbors—reflect the spirit and the ingenuity people had during the Depression," he philosophized in his later years.

"But it was really not all that great. Indeed, while families were brought closer together and so on, some monstrous human catastrophes occurred during that time. Farmers, right and left, lost their farms. Some people who had to declare bankruptcy shot themselves. And there were countless other tragedies. It was a style of life so different, so alien from what we know today, that it's hard to conceive it even happened in the same country where we now live."

Things did not look up for the Rautenstrauses until late in 1934 when Christian accepted the ministry of a much larger parish, St. John's Lutheran in Russell, Kansas. It was a major promotion. The brick church was huge compared with the two he had served in Nebraska, as was the parson's house. The euphoria, however, would be relatively short lived. As reported in the *St. John Congregational History*, "The Great Depression did not significantly touch Russell until 1935 when a severe drought caused total crop failure. Pastor Rautenstraus led the congregation through this period of depression, which was characterized by severe dust storms that devastated the spirits of even the most optimistic individuals. St. John experienced no growth in membership during the 1930s."

Adding to the problems of Russell's declining economy and keeping his parishioner's spirits up, Rev. and Mrs. Rautenstraus had to deal with some personal milestones as well. The year 1936 would produce two memorable family events, one blissful and gay, and the other sad and terrible. The happy affair would be the marriage of Christian and Emma's only daughter Ruth to Jay Dumler. The tragedy would involve their oldest son.

Located on the central plains of Kansas, Russell is halfway between the Smoky Hill and Saline Rivers, just off present-day Interstate I-70. It is in the heart of what is known as "the land of the post rock"—fence posts made from quarried limestone slabs because of the shortage of timber in the area (in the early days of its settlement). Not a town known for its bustling economy, Russell has remained small. Its population in 1996 was 7,835.

This rural setting fit like a glove for a young, pre-teenage boy like Roland. With his older siblings away at college or working, he was left alone a lot more and he freely enjoyed his space. In the late 1970s, he took up kayaking on waterways around Boulder because he recalled how relaxing it was as a youth in Russell. It allowed him time alone to gather his thoughts. The reflective times he spent boating and rafting, alone or with pals, (on the Smoky Hill and Saline tributaries) left a strong impression on Rautenstraus for life.

Volga-Germans from Russia homesteaded, settled and improved much of the rich farm land in the Russell region. Many had come to the land of "milk and honey" to make their fortunes, enticed by romantic tales spread by agents of the Kansas Pacific and Union Pacific railroads. These first and second-generation immigrants were hard working, rigidly faithful to their religions and clannish—isolation-ists—by nature. Catholics tended to have little to do with non-Catholics. Lutherans were the same. In Russia, Volga-Germans never mingled with nor married their Russian neighbors. They even prided themselves on not learning Russian though most lived along the Volga River for more than 100 years. A strong, solid German-speaking theologian like Rev. Christian Rautenstraus fit their needs to a tee. But not all of churchgoers to St. John spoke only German.

There was a growing discord between the parish's German-speaking and English-speaking members, whose numbers were increasing. "Pastor Rautenstraus," it was written in the *Congregational History*, "could preach in English, but with a heavy German accent that many found difficult to understand. The language conflict continued during his pastorate at St. John. There was opposition [to Christian] from the supporters of English who could not understand his English sermons."

But Rautenstraus was creative, which helped keep him entrenched at his post. To avoid any misunderstandings at public events—like confirmation ceremonies—he used sign language. "So that no one would be embarrassed, he established a method by which each confirmand could signal if he or she knew the answer to his question. Thumbs up meant they knew; thumbs down meant they didn't." The *Congregational History* additionally pointed out, "In spite of the hardships of the Great Depression—when lives, families and fortunes were falling apart—St. John church members remained loyal and never missed paying the pastor's salary."

Around the time his family relocated to Russell, Herbert moved to Fort Collins, Colorado, and enrolled at what is now Colorado State University (CSU) to earn a degree in forestry. After years of struggling to make money and find the time, Rev. Rautenstraus' oldest son graduated from college on June 4, 1936 with a bachelor of science degree. A week later he died of cancer. He had just celebrated his 25th birthday in May. His death left the Rautenstraus family stunned, heart broken and devastated. Roland, at 12—about the same age his father was when he was orphaned—would begin his last year of junior high school with a heavy heart. He had lost the big brother he idolized. This event brought him even closer to his sister Ruth.

It was a different situation with Roland and his brother Walter. They never felt real close to each other, according to Walter's son Kent. "My dad and uncle Rolie probably wouldn't have had much to do with each other or been friends if they hadn't been brothers." He recalled his father saying Roland was always getting in the way and being a nuisance when they were growing up—not an uncommon feeling among siblings with a wide age gap between them. Raut's son Curt felt that even though the two brothers did not have an overwhelming amount of things in common they enjoyed each other's company. "My dad and Walt always got along pretty well," he said.

With Kansas beginning to shake off the effects of the Depression, young Roland started blossoming, first in junior high then high school. He began showing signs of special talents in elocution and debate, and athletics. A confident and grown-up young fellow, he was already bigger than his father, several inches taller and more powerfully built. He was starting to develop into a football star.

During the 1938-39 school year when he was a sophomore, Roland was a member of the four-person Russell High School debate team. It won the state debate championship and earned Raut a trophy the size of a table lamp. The next year, as a junior, he not only won the Kansas Class A state debate championship trophy (another monster-sized piece), but received a personal letter of congratulations from Governor Payne Ratner and offers for speaking engagements from local service clubs. Heady stuff for a 15 year old. He was the January guest speaker for the Kiwanis International Club of Russell, kicking off its 1939 season.

Around this time, young Rautenstraus began a life-long friendship with Robert Joseph Dole (one day to become a U.S. Senator, president of the Senate and the 1996 Republican Party candidate for president). As pals in junior high, the two of them—along with another buddy, Bob Smith—had signed a "sacred pact" concerning their decorum, behavior and the language they used around girls. (See Appendix B.)

In addition to Bob Dole, Roland began a lasting relationship with another junior high and high school classmate, the county judge's son, Philip Ruppenthal. Curt Rautenstraus said Phil was his father's best friend in high school. He recalled how much Raut enjoyed getting together with Dole and Ruppenthal during excursions to the east coast over the years, especially for the Orange Bowl games in which CU played. Both Dole and Ruppenthal had homes in Florida, the site of the New Year's day event. Phil was the first Russell native son to graduate from Harvard. (CU made its first Orange Bowl appearance January 1, 1957, defeating Clemson 27-21.)

Roland's sister Ruth was one of his—as well as Dole's and Ruppenthal's—school teachers. Russell, Kansas, for as small as it was, turned out a record number of notable characters. Ruth's son Larry Dumler said his mother would often list her famous students, including two U.S. senators (Dole and Arlen Spector), a university president (Raut), a highly successful businessman (Ruppenthal) and a billionaire (Philip Anshutz).

During Roland's junior year in high school, Rev. Rautenstraus' health was frail, and the family had not fully recovered from the loss of Herbert. Doctors suggested it would be best if he took a rest from the ministry. Both of his older children—Ruth and Walter—had moved and were living in the Denver area. When Walter invited his father to come help with his poultry business in Colorado, Christian thought it a good idea and he agreed. He was 57 years old and had been ministering, without a break, for 30 years. He and Emma made plans to once again pull up stakes and move, this time to colorful Colorado—a favorite family vacation spot for years.

Roland wanted to stay in Russell to finish his last year of high school and pleaded with his parents to do so, with no success. In the spring of 1940, the reverend's youngest son bid his Kansas school chums good-bye and embarked, with his parents, on a new adventure to Wheat Ridge at the foot of the majestic Rocky Mountains. He would soon call Colorado home, never to leave it for any length of time, for the rest of his life.

3

WHEAT RIDGE
(1940-1942)

I f Roland missed his old high school buddies back in
Russell or felt out of place in his new surroundings, he
did not give any signs of it. Nor did he complain about
having to finish his last year of high school in a new place
with new faces and classmates. Just the opposite seemed
to be the case. Always confident and outgoing, he adapted
quickly and made friends easily.

Wheat Ridge High, in those days, was not as big as
Russell High and young Rautenstraus quickly fit in. He
was a bigger fish in a smaller pond, especially on the football field. He became a first stringer at guard within days
after going out for the team, which had high hopes of re-
peating as champions of the Central Suburban League.

The reverend's entire clan—Ruth, her husband Jay
Dumler, their son Larry, bachelor Walter, Emma and
Roland, and himself—was now living in Wheat Ridge. The
memory of Herbert's sudden passing still lingered and they
felt some consolation being together. Ruth was always a
calming force, greatly respected and admired by the whole
family. Roland, especially, was pleased to be living close to
her again. "Ruth had the greatest influence on my dad of

anyone in his family. She was college educated and smart," said Raut's son Curt.

George Maler, who would one day become Rautenstraus' college roommate in Boulder, does not remember him ever discussing his parents or his brother (while they were roommates). But he recalled many occasions when Raut talked warmly and proudly about his sister. It was almost as if Ruth—12 years his senior—was Roland's surrogate mother. "My mother kind of raised Raut," agreed her son Larry. "My grandparents had this old-world upbringing. They were strict, in a moral sense, not in a physical sense. So was my mother. All three had strong moral ethics. None of them, though, were demonstrative about showing their emotions."

Jay Dumler's auto parts venture was proving to be successful, which provided Ruth with enough security and stability to continue her nurturing ways. "Ruth, when I first met her (in 1942), lived in this big house on 38th Avenue and Roland was so proud of her. Everyone was very fond of her. She was an extremely nice person—a very interesting lady. And you could tell she cared a lot about Roland and what he planned to do," said Willie Atler, who was his college sweetheart.

Larry was 14 years younger than Roland—about the same age difference as between Ruth and Roland. He recalled, "Raut stayed with us for a while after he came back from the war." Dumler, who eventually became a physician and practiced at the Boulder Medical Center, added, "He would come over to the house—before and after he was married—and we would play catch or toss the football around. He was always interested in my education, what I wanted to do with my life."

When Christian and Emma's children were growing up, the family often vacationed in the Estes Park area. Retiring in Colorado was something they had often talked about. Following his doctor's recommendation to get some rest, the reverend's retirement came a little earlier than he had planned, and he discovered he was not quite ready for it. Nor was helping his son Walter with his poultry business quite what he had in mind. Shortly after he arrived in Wheat Ridge, a call came from the Emanuel Lutheran Church in Hoisington, Kansas—only 30 miles from his old parish in Russell—and the reverend quickly agreed to come out of early retirement to be its pastor.

Wheat Ridge, in the early 1940s, was a bucolic small rural town on the outskirts of Denver. Like Arvada up the road, it was the town center for a series of dairy, poultry, vegetable and other specialty farms. Many were owned and/or operated by immigrants—Germans, Italians and others of European origin. Some operations were as small as five acres and their crops were as diversified as the people. Many shipped their wares nationwide; a few were well-known brands like Davis carnations and Wilmore nursery stock (trees and shrubs).

The physical setting of the area differed little from where the Rautenstrauses had come, except that a bustling big city was just a hop-and-skip away to the southeast, and the massive Rockies towered to the west of them. The climate was dry and the air fresh and crisp. Many thought it an ideal place to live. But Emma and Christian's first stay there came and went quickly. Any roots they—or their youngest son—may have planted in Wheat Ridge were short lived and shallow. Few of the high school friends Roland stayed in close contact with throughout his adult years came from there. More of them originated in Russell.

Frank Seeton, whose family lived a block down the street from the Rautenstrauses, said, "Roland and I would often walk to school together." Frank—a year behind Roland in school—was a starter on the Wheat Ridge High

School football team along with Raut. The two of them, he said, "talked mostly football talk when we walked home after football practice." Though this transplant from Russell was popular, he was not in the inner circle of Frank's friends nor anyone else's. He had not been in town long enough to make long-lasting relationships with anyone. Seeton could not remember ever being in Roland's home during high school, though he had Roland over to his house occasionally with some other school pals.

Seeton, who would graduate from the Colorado School of Mines as a mining engineer, said that Raut never talked about his parents or his siblings with him or anyone else he knew. He did, though, remember young Rautenstraus telling him, with pride, that he had been on the championship oratory team in Kansas. "He [Raut] was a good speaker. But we didn't have a program like that at Wheat Ridge, so he couldn't display that talent in a formal way," recalled Frank. "But he wasn't shy about speaking out and was good at it. We all considered him the school's best talker and story teller."

Joe Finley, a tackle playing next to Rautenstraus on the line of the school's football team, noted, "He [Raut] could use words most of us couldn't even understand." Seeton added, "He was a first-class guy. He was a big, nice-looking kid and he never had any trouble dating girls."

Gladys (Cameron) DiLorenzo said, "I had this mad crush on Rolie. I was just a sophomore so we never dated, but he was so good-looking—and charming. A lot of my [girl] friends thought of him the same way but he only dated girls who were juniors or seniors." Gladys, who was a Wheat Ridge cheerleader, also recalled that "Rolie was quite smitten by Glennie Perry and he once got in a fight over her with Pal Anderson. Glennie and Rolie never did get together though." Anderson and Rautenstraus, however, became friends. Both ended up at CU, played together on its football team and became naval officers serving overseas. Pal was among the handful of Wheat Ridge High graduates who stayed in contact with Rautenstraus throughout his career. He grinned when he recalled their high school fisticuffs, "It was the last fight I ever had, and I think it was Rolie's too."

One of the girls who dated Roland at Wheat Ridge, Shirley (Gauthier) Downs, recalled, "He was a cute guy and so witty. I sat across from him in lit class and one day he dared me to learn the poem, 'The Raven.' I took the dare and recited it to him in a few days word for word—and it was six pages long! He was impressed and we started going out together." When asked if he talked about his family on their dates, she replied, "I knew his family had a chicken farm and delivered eggs but I never knew his father was a minister [until much later in the 1990s]."

After Roland left Wheat Ridge High, Shirley lost track of him. "The war got in the way of things. Lots of Wheat Ridge boys died in it." When Rautenstraus became president of CU, their paths crossed again. While she worked for former Congresswoman Pat Schroeder, her office had several dealings with the University, mainly on minority issues.

Frank Seeton's mining career took him around the world, but in the late 1960s his offices were in the Denver Club Building in downtown Denver. Once during that time, he and Rautenstraus bumped into each other on 16th Street by happenstance. The two former neighbors and football teammates exchanged pleasantries, promised to have lunch together sometime, but never did. Frank said that, even though he—and most everyone else from their high school days—greatly admired their old classmate's accomplishments, they rarely got together with Roland—"only at a few school reunions." Said Seeton, "I talked with several people who visited him at his big office in Boulder when he was president. And they were impressed, especially with how gracious, approachable and generous with his time he was, even though they hadn't seen him for years."

Rautenstraus usually went out of his way to be helpful to any old, long-lost school acquaintance, no matter what the request. The fullback on the Wheat Ridge team, Jack Davis, once asked him about getting tickets to the CU-Minnesota football game. Davis—from the Davis carnations clan—was one of the richest kids in school in 1941. "He had a brand new car every year in high school," said Seeton. In the 1970s, he was no longer rich. He had a farm and lived in Minnesota. "Raut," Davis recounted, "not only got me tickets on the 50 yard line, but invited me to meet with the regents and attend a couple of parties. It was a big deal. He was an extremely generous man."

Another time in the 1970s, when Gladys DiLorenzo's son was struggling to get into dental school at Creighton University in Nebraska, she contacted Rautenstraus. "I called Rolie about Scotty [her son] and he had us come up to his office. He was such a busy man with big problems to solve and I hadn't seen him for 30 some years. Yet, he took the time to help us. He told Scotty different things to do and how to go about getting accepted in graduate school. He even wrote a letter of recommendation for him. My son—who one year later got into Creighton—thought Rolie was the greatest. Rolie was such a tolerant person, especially with young people. He could relate to all age groups so well."

Roland was one of the youngest kids in his class when he graduated from Wheat Ridge High on May 28, 1941. He had turned 17 just three months before. Yet, the sandy haired, blue-eyed lad, with the unforgettable voice, had been chosen to deliver the speech at his class' commencement exercise, which he did with excellence. Shortly thereafter, Roland received a congratulatory letter from Superintendent of Schools Paul Stevens complimenting him on his "fine presentation."

Stevens further wrote, "I was indeed proud of you and the excellent manner in which you represented your school. I compliment you highly on your all-around ability and especially your ability as a student speaker. We will miss you a lot next year. Remember, you have gained your recognition by doing more than was required of you. Continue to make the most of every opportunity that comes your way. Keep your high ideals of accomplishment and character ever before you. It is my wish that you find happiness and success in whatever line of work you may wish to pursue."

It was heady stuff, certainly an ego-building letter to encourage—and challenge—any young man's personal pursuits for the future.

Further pumping up his confidence, on July 1, 1941, he received an official letter from the chairman of the All-Star Game Committee, N.C. Morris. It invited him to participate in the first annual Colorado All-Star Football Game to be played at Denver University stadium on August 22, 1941. He had been notified earlier of his selection to the state all-star football team but the letter verified he would play in the All-Star game, at a big college stadium, no less.

Prior to and in addition to these all-state honors, he had been selected by both *The Denver Post* and the *Rocky Mountain News* as all-conference guard from the Central Suburban Football League. A 5'-11", 180-pound lineman, he was one of the larger high school players of his day. Seeton, a halfback on Rautenstraus' Wheat Ridge team—he was named all-conference at that position in 1942—said, "In those days, halfbacks weighed 150 pounds while linemen were 20 pounds or so bigger. Roland—who was a pulling guard—was even bigger and he opened up some nice-sized holes for me and the other backs to run through."

The August All-Star Game would expose Roland, for the first time, to big-time college football coaches. The lead coach for his football squad—he was on the Denver Metropolitan Area team playing the State (at large) team—was E.E. "Tad" Wieman, Princeton University's famous coach. Assisting Wieman were local high school coaches, Pat Panek of East, Frank Mielens of West and Fritz S. Brennecke of Golden. Brennecke and Rautenstraus would be reunited, through some unlikely circumstances, three decades and three years later.

The game itself ended as a low-scoring affair, to say the least, with most of the offensive movement occurring between, but not over, the goal lines. Wayne Hyllegard (from Golden High School) kicked a 30-yard field goal for the Denver Metro team in the fourth quarter, the only points scored by either team, giving the Metro-Denver team a 3 to 0 win. Played before a crowd of 7,702 paying customers, *The Denver Post* (August 23, 1941) proclaimed, "Denver outplayed State in all departments of the game except punting." The reporter apparently did not feel the score adequately reflected the "dominance" of the contest by the "local boys."

The fall of 1941 found Roland in Las Vegas working on a survey crew for the railroad and as a part-time card dealer at one of the rough-and-tumble town's newly opened casinos. According to his son Curt, he had planned on attending Denver University earlier but changed his mind at the last minute. He had also tried to enlist in the Navy's elite officers program right out of high school but was put off, because of his age.

Las Vegas was a temporary stop as Roland bided his time and contemplated his next move. It allowed him to make and accumulate some money. And, just possibly, get out of his surroundings and see some different parts of the country before he would be accepted into the service. Not completely removed from his mind at the time, though, was the idea of going to Colorado's "teachers' college" in Greeley—what is now called the University of Northern Colorado (UNC)—to be a psychologist or a teacher, majoring in literature or history. The school had offered him a football scholarship but it was not enough to cover all of his costs. Some time off from school to earn enough money to bankroll a year at UNC seemed like the ticket for the young lad with big dreams.

By the summer of 1942, the U.S. was totally engrossed in WWII and wartime rationing was commonplace. Rev. and Mrs. Rautenstraus were back in Kansas at his new parish, which had a predominately German-speaking congregation. It relieved Christian of having to prepare his sermons in two languages. He only had to conduct his services in German, a break from his last assignment at Russell. Their move, however, left Roland without a home base in Colorado and he re-contacted the Navy. "I enlisted in a program the Navy initially called V1 then V12," Raut told Pam Penfold in a 1996 interview.* "They didn't have the program ready so they said go to college and we'll call you when we're ready." With that in mind he finalized plans to enter UNC in the fall.

The first time Willie Atler laid eyes on Roland Rautenstraus he was *a* sight, with a big gash across his forehead. But the pretty and petite brunette—born in Oklahoma City, raised in Pueblo and graduated from Lakewood High School—was impressed by the big freshman football player. He was quite good-looking, personable and easy to talk to. She had been apprehensive about meeting him, at first. A friend from her high school, a practical joker and

---

*The September 1996 conversations Rautenstraus had with Penfold, editor of *The Coloradan*—a CU-Boulder Alumni Association publication—was the last, in-depth interview he had with the media. He was 72 at the time.

also a football player, had arranged the meeting. But once she got to know Roland, she learned he was on some kind of a scholarship and remembered hearing the president (of UNC) saying about her new beau, "It's nice to have someone with both brains and brawn."

After their initial rendezvous—sharing a booth at the UNC student union—Willie and Roland continued to see each other on a regular basis. On their first official date, they went into downtown Greeley and ended up in the Montgomery Ward department store. The store was in the process of changing the prices on virtually everything in the place and it was a "zoo." Willie and Raut mischievously changed a few of its price tags as well. "It was a really silly and careless thing to do, but that's what we did (giggling all the time). After that we just started dating on a regular basis," she said.

During this time, she remembered, Raut had "no intention of ever being an engineer." He, like she, had enrolled at UNC the fall of 1942 to become a teacher. She was being supported by her mother and stepfather. Roland, she recalled, "was on a football scholarship but it wasn't much. He had a little money from his days working in Las Vegas, but he had to work part-time at the school to make ends meet."

His exploits on the college gridiron continued to be noteworthy, a continuation of his high school days. He made the football team as a guard, the same position he played at Wheat Ridge. UNC came in second place in the Rocky Mountain Conference in 1942. Rautenstraus, though only a freshman, was named Honorable Mention on *The Denver Post's* All-RMC Team that same year. He had not grown much since he was in high school and, though he was considered good sized for a high school lineman, he had to use cunning as much as strength in the college ranks.

At least one of his friends, though, thought him to be a pretty tough fellow in his own right: his college roommate, Earl (Shep) Shepard. Years after their time together in Greeley, Shep would tell people that, pound for pound, "Rolie was the strongest man he'd ever met." Shep served as Roland's best-man at his wedding in 1946 and the two would remain close friends for life, even though they lived in different parts of the country.

Just like with his Russell high school buddies, Raut would—throughout his life—stay in close touch with Shepard. When he traveled around the country, he would stop to see whoever was living in the city he was visiting. On the east coast, that was usually Bob Dole in Washington, DC or Phil Ruppenthal in Florida. On the west coast it was Shep, who eventually became a publisher in San Diego.

Before his first year at UNC ended, young Rautenstraus had heard from the Navy. He was officially accepted in their officers program. The only hitch: the program he was selected for was being offered either in Colorado Springs at Colorado College or in Boulder at the University of Colorado. And they wanted to educate and train engineers.

4

NAVAL OFFICER
(1943-1946)

The fall of 1943 found 19-year-old Roland Rautenstraus enrolled in the Navy's V-12 officer's training program at the University of Colorado and a member of the school's football team. He also faced a consequential alteration to his plans for a life's career. The Navy needed engineers for the war effort, and Raut, at the Navy's suggestion, had changed his major from arts and science to engineering. He had enrolled in the College of Engineering and—not without misgivings from his father who had hoped Roland would become a theologian like himself or a school teacher like his sister Ruth—matriculated to become a civil engineer.

It was during this time that Roland met—and became familiar with—two men who instilled in him a deep appreciation for the profession he had just chosen. One was Warren Raeder, the new head of the civil engineering department, a position Rautenstraus himself would one day hold, and the other was Clarence L. Eckel, the new dean of the College of Engineering. Each had only recently been appointed to his position; Raeder assuming the one Eckel had held for nearly 20 years (1926-43).

Of the two, Eckel had the most influence and was the more capable mentor on Raut's extraordinary path. Both were strong, rigid and unemotional men, not unlike Roland's father. Physically, Raeder even looked, surprisingly, a bit like Christian Rautenstraus.

An alumnus of North High School in Denver, Eckel had strong Colorado roots. He entered the University in 1910, becoming an engineering honor student and an All-Rocky Mountain Conference center on the football team. He graduated in 1914 and immediately joined the civil engineering faculty as an instructor. He served at the front in the engineering battalion of the National Guard in WWI. After the war, he spent four years at the University of Pennsylvania before returning to Colorado in 1923 as a professor. As reported by William Davis in *Glory Colorado!*, the no-nonsense Eckel, "admitted [in 1947] to only one hobby—the College of Engineering." Another passion was his support of local engineering associations that, as will be discussed later, was almost fanatical.

Roland and Willie continued to date even though he now lived in Boulder and she remained at college in Greeley. She sometimes went to Denver by bus or train. He would catch a ride with a couple of guys who had cars—or he would hitchhike—and they would meet there. Other times he would hitchhike from Boulder to Greeley to see her on weekends and "stay in the dorms," Willie recalled, "with some fellows he knew."

Boulder—beautifully nestled into the foothills of the Rockies—was, in those days, a small, unassuming town of 13,000 (mostly) peaceful souls. The awe-inspiring rock face of the Flatirons formation loomed above the CU campus, which was on a hill south of Boulder's town center. During

WWII, the University was swarming with students dressed in military uniforms.

Rautenstraus lived on campus near historic Macky Auditorium and Varsity Lake in the Harding Wing of Sewall Residence Hall, a women's dormitory taken over by the Navy for the war effort. It was a relatively new structure at the time—built in 1934—a handsome red sandstone building. The structure was a classic example, according to CU-Boulder campus architect Bill Deno, of "Tuscan vernacular" architecture, initiated by Charles Klauder. It typified the "rural Italian" style beginning to dramatically change and unify the look of the sprawling CU campus.

Roland's roommate George Maler, an electrical engineering major who was also enrolled in the V-12 program, remembered how sometimes six students stayed in a room designed to hold two. Their room had two mirrors on the wall. George remembered how Raut, always trying to improve his elocution, would position himself to see in the mirrors while speaking so he could practice his delivery and stage presence. Also strong in his memory was Roland's toughness—how he played a few football games even though he had a broken wrist, which was in a cast.

Maler, who ultimately became the associate dean of engineering (from 1966 to 1986), was dating his future wife, Marge, at the time. Roland was going with Willie. They would often double date. Many a time it meant sharing a long, tiring car trip to Denver. The Denver-Boulder Turnpike did not exist then and people had to take the slow-moving back roads to get between the two places. Another engineering student in the V-12 program who often joined Maler and Rautenstraus on their treks to Denver—because he was dating a young lady in the Denver area—was Al Swanson. He became a consulting engineer and founded Swanson and Rink, one of the largest mechanical and electrical engineering firms in the Rocky Mountain Region.

At Rautenstraus' farewell party when he retired as CU's 12th president in 1980, Maler recalled "those Saturday afternoons hitchhiking into Denver (with Raut and Al) to meet three gorgeous girls—Marge, Willie and Bonna—for an evening of wining, dining and dancing," They frequented the old Elitch's Trocadero Ballroom in Wheat Ridge. Nationally known bands led by the likes of Eddie Howard and Dick Jurgens often played there in those days.

After WWII, all three men married their college sweethearts. George and Roland continued their close friendship until the early 1980s. Then things between them changed dramatically.

Not all of Rautenstraus' life-long friendships from his student days at CU were developed through the V-12 program. Some of his college friends were civilians. Ed Haase (BSCE '44)—who became the chief engineer for the Colorado Highway Department—said their relationship came about because they "frequented the same civil engineering classes." Haase was a big fan of CU football and was impressed that one of his classmates starred on the team. "Roland always wore his sailor uniform to class, but so did all the rest of the navy officer-candidates. What made him stand out was that he had so much charisma. He was 'one of the guys' and everyone just plain enjoyed being around him. He was an exciting person and that persona remained with him throughout his life."

Football was, indeed, a big part of Roland's college days. It is no surprise that the strong, strapping and athletic young man continued to be a stand-out in the sport. It did not matter that Colorado was a larger and more competitive place than the smaller college at Greeley. Rautenstraus himself was a little heavier, at 185 pounds, than when he starred at UNC. His position on CU's team was the same one he had played since high school: guard. He lettered at the sport both years he played in Boulder—

1943 and 1944. In his senior year, he was named captain of the team for the Peru State (a college in Nebraska) game on November 11, 1944. Colorado won the game 40-12 and Raut was given the game ball. It became one of his son Curt's most prized possessions—from when he was a small boy to today.

Rautenstraus played football in the days when college athletes played on both squads and, from all accounts, he was as good on defense as he was on offense. In a 1943 newspaper account about the October 16 game against a tough Salt Lake City Airbase team, he was singled out for blocking a punt near the goal line that led to the go-ahead touchdown. It helped Colorado rally and put the game on ice, with CU winning 14-0. It was the team's fourth straight victory of the year.

In 1943, Raut's coach was gentlemanly Jim Yeager, by then in his third season. With a limited conference schedule because of WWII, the team only played seven games, with five wins and two losses. Both defeats came against Colorado College, whose team, like Colorado's, predominately consisted of V-12 Naval and Marine Corps officer candidates.

The venerable and legendary track coach Frank Potts, who also served as the interim football coach in 1940, filled in for Yeager when he was called into the armed services in 1944. It was Raut's last year as a Colorado football player and this time CU trounced Colorado College twice: 28-0 and 40-6. The 1944 record was 6 wins against 2 losses and, as in the previous year, the team's schedule was limited because of the war.

Yeager and Potts, each in his own distinctive way, must have had a significant impact on young Rautenstraus as well as countless other young men they coached. Both were outstanding collegiate athletes and classic role models. Yeager, a former Kansas State star, successfully coached at Iowa State prior to coming to Colorado. His 1938 Cyclones were undefeated before losing to Oklahoma 10-0 for the Big Six title. Called "Gentleman Jim" he was an immensely popular and highly regarded coach, a fine person and a good leader. His arrival on the CU scene was ushered in with great excitement and anticipation. Many a young man, including Raut, learned much about the value of teamwork from him.

Frank Potts was an all-conference fullback and a national pole vault champion at the University of Oklahoma. Potts, who specialized in coaching track and field, was inducted into the Colorado Sports Hall of Fame in 1970. During his 41-year career at Colorado, he produced 19 All-American athletes and captured 10 Rocky Mountain Conference team championships. When inducted into the Colorado Hall of Fame, he said that the rewards of his career were "in sharing the successes of athletes both on and off the field, and in being associated with so many outstanding people involved in sports."

In 1944, Rautenstraus was selected by the International News Service to its All-Rockies football team and was named guard on its Honorable Mention team. Coach Potts didn't know in 1970 when he accepted his Hall of Fame designation that, one day, one of his athletes' off-the-field successes would include becoming the president of the University that Potts so dearly loved.

Walt Koelbel (BS Bus '47), one of Raut's teammates on the 1944 football team, said, "Raut was a tough competitor, he loved the game. We played some very good service clubs back then, with big, strong players—some All-Americans. And even though he wasn't all that big, Raut always more than held his own."

Now a successful commercial real estate developer and builder in Denver, Koelbel, who was also in the V-12 program with Roland, recalled how Rautenstraus—after he became a professor—often invited Walt to lecture his students. "Raut wanted them to learn about the real life situations engineers encountered in the business world."

By the start of 1945, the U.S. armed forces in the Pacific Theater—where many of the V-12 trainees were slated to go—were announcing major victories and making significant progress in their campaign to invade Japan. When "Old Glory" was raised on Iwo Jima on February 23, the Naval and Marine officers-to-be at the University of Colorado wondered if they would ever make it into action; and if they would have any meaningful effect on American's final push to end the war.

To further add to these uncertainties, on April 30 Adolf Hitler, the maniacal force behind the war in the European Theater, crazed over Germany's impending defeat, committed suicide. Within 10 days, the Germans were at the table to sign an unconditional surrender. Only the U.S. troops in the Pacific remained at war.

News of the U.S. and Allied Forces' victories, however, did not come without word of personal tragedies as well. Few of the officer candidates did not have someone—a friend, relative or loved one—who was not in harm's way. Many were touched by losses: news of deaths, permanent injuries and/or someone being lost in action.

Rautenstraus mostly heard reports concerning school chums from high school and college. In 1996, during one of his last in-depth interviews, Roland recounted to Pam Penfold (editor of *The Coloradan*), "The number of people I knew who died [in WWII] is considerable. They were very good people and it isn't fair that they had to die, or that others had to be seriously disabled.

"Take my friend Bob Dole: to be injured in the war the way he was is heartbreaking. When we were boys together in Kansas, he was our school's star athlete—and he was quite handsome. All the girls were absolutely gaga about him, but he was too shy to even talk to them. Now he's running for president and isn't shy about getting up in front of thousands and thousands of people. It's remarkable how he overcame the physical disabilities he incurred on the battlefield to be where he is today. But it's so sad he, and others, had to pay the price they did for us to win the war."

Suddenly, on August 6, 1945, the U.S. dropped an atomic bomb on Hiroshima, Japan. Two days later, a second one was dropped on Nagasaki. On August 15, Japan surrendered.

With WWII essentially over, Rautenstraus and other soon-to-be-officers must have had mixed feelings in the fall of 1945. They were sent to Providence, Rhode Island, for the last stages of their indoctrination and formal installation as officers in the U.S. Navy. A dashing and dapper lot in their full dress uniforms, they showed up at a time when the country was jubilant that the weary and bloody war was over. They surely fluttered the hearts of many young ladies on the eastern seaboard as they were put "on display" at commencement exercises.

After receiving his commission as assistant civil engineer with the rank of ensign, 21-year-old Roland Rautenstraus was shipped out to Okinawa for mop-up operations. A number of renegade Japanese soldiers remained in the hills of the island and had to be dealt with. And a lot of roads, airfield runways and harbors needed to be constructed and/or repaired. What an exciting time and adventure it must have been for young men from the small towns and rural areas of America to be working overseas for the first time, in a place many of them never knew existed before WWII. It was the first time Rautenstraus was put in charge of and supervised major construction work.

"Our construction battalion," recalled Raut, "consisted of an interesting group of people: 30 and 40-year-old experienced construction workers and the officer corps who were all kids—civil engineering graduates without any significant experience with construction. It was interesting how well we blended together and got along. They respected us for our engineering abilities and we them for their construction knowledge and skill. In particular, we really admired a guy who was good at using construction tools or operating equipment.

"When a 20-year-old is given authority and put in charge of people who know what they are doing—as the Navy's Seabees did—he or she learns a lot. Plus, you learn a lot about yourself: what you can handle and what you can't." What he learned about stabilizing soils would be put to use in the 1960s when he would be a consultant to the highway department in Colorado.

Most Seabees who served on Okinawa during WWII report that building on the island during this time required not only skill with using construction equipment but creativity in dealing with its environmental conditions. Frequent rains—and an occasional hurricane—turned the island's clays into a sticky muck that was unbelievably frustrating to work with and build on. Trucks and other heavy equipment seemed to be constantly mired in it. The Seabees came up with ways to stabilize the mud using coral quarried from the ocean. And they learned new ways to keep engines and themselves dry. Keeping their socks and shoes from rotting—and their skin free of sores—took a major effort. Staying out of the rifle sights of Japanese snipers who lingered on the islands was another.

During his tour of duty in the Pacific, a breathtaking incident occurred that profoundly affected R. C. Rautenstraus for the rest of his days. When discussing the event in his later years, Raut would muse, "It's during those kinds of experiences that you learn what scares you and what doesn't."

Several slightly different versions of Raut's Okinawa incident have been told, each with certain colorful variations made to the story. The basic facts, however, remain constant. One of his outfit's operations required that they fly materials (in one version, rolls of copper wire or pipe) from one island to another. On this particular flight, Raut fell through an open door—and nearly to his death. While pushing the material out the door, his safety harness got caught and he was sucked out of the airplane.

Somehow his harness stayed connected to the plane, keeping him from free falling. He was, however, dragged, flopping in the wind, behind the airplane while the pilot maneuvered around and around. It took nearly 15 minutes before Raut's crew could pull him back inside to safety. As the craft headed for home base, it developed engine trouble and crash landed into the sea.

For the next 30 years, Roland refused to get into an airplane. And when he finally did, because his position as president of the University demanded it, he was "never a happy flier" according to his wife Willie.

The rest of his duty—which he spent on the ground or the water—was not as life-threatening but just as thrilling, nevertheless. General Douglas MacArthur, the Supreme Commander of Allied Forces in the Pacific and hero to many, had just begun the occupation and reconstruction of Japan and its environs. This was precisely the kind of activity the Seabees were trained to do. It was a once-in-a-lifetime opportunity that gave the Navy's young engineers a view of what post-WWII construction would to be like globally.

Discharged from active duty in the Spring of 1946, Lieutenant Rautenstraus did not waste any time getting back to Colorado. He returned home from the Pacific by ship, then train. He was safely back in Boulder by May, in time for Willie's graduation from Greeley with a degree in teaching.

They had kept their romance alive through the mail. "He wrote great letters, wonderful letters," she said. They married on June 30, 1946 and, being the worldly man he now was, Roland promised to take her places she had never seen, just as soon as he finished work for his engineering degree. He had no intention of being a college professor nor staying in Boulder. He wanted to conquer the big world out there.

However, he still had a few credit hours to finish for his bachelor's degree and Dean Eckel needed instructors to handle the heavy influx of engineering students expected back from the war. So a deal was struck. He hired Raut, beginning in the fall quarter of 1946, to teach while finishing his course work at a salary of $150 a quarter. Starting in September, Willie also had a job teaching at Longmont High School—at a whopping salary of $1,700 a year. (One of her prize students during her time at Longmont was astronaut Vance Brand, who later piloted the Apollo command module during the Apollo-Soyuz space mission.)

In the summer of 1946, life looked promising for the happy, handsome, young couple as they left for their honeymoon in Mexico.

5

AFTER THE WAR
(1946-1963)

Right after WWII, there was a lot of talk, planning and scheming underway to connect Denver and Boulder by surface with a more direct route. Civil engineering professors from the University worked with state highway and local officials on designs for such a connection. White-haired and stately Roderic Downing, often called the father of the project, was a major participant. His right hand man, one of the college's youngest faculty members, was a confident and well-spoken former Naval officer just back from road building with the Seabees in the Pacific.

Rautenstraus was forever proud of—and vocal about—his involvement in the design of the Denver-Boulder Turnpike (U.S. 36), which was not without its naysayers and critics. Some thought it folly and doubted the toll road would ever pay for itself when it opened on January 19, 1952.

The project, though, quickly proved to be a sound investment. The toll station located at the Broomfield turnoff took its last collection on September 14, 1967, well ahead of schedule. The Turnpike has enormously impacted transportation, growth patterns and history, not only in Boulder but in all the communities along its path.

Building the Turnpike remained one of Rautenstraus' favorite topics in his highway engineering design class up to the last day he taught. Lindsay Corotis (BSCE '99), one of the students to take the final course he ever taught — Transportation Engineering—remembered how, even at age 73 and after discussing it for 45 years, Raut's face brightened when he talked about its conception and significance to the state. He knew it wasn't perfect—and that it would be under-designed for tomorrow's traffic—but it was far reaching for its time.

John Buechner (the University's current president) recalled a time in the 1970s when he and Raut, still president and his boss, were on their way to meet with legislators at the Capitol. Traffic was jammed up at the I-25 and Turnpike Interchange. John, frustrated, said, "I wonder who the idiot was who designed this thing?" And calmly Raut replied, "Jonathan*, I did."

Rautenstraus received his Bachelor of Science in Civil Engineering at the end of the fall quarter in 1946 when he was 22 years old. Less than a year later, he was officially appointed as a full time Instructor in civil engineering by Vice President W. F. Dyde at a "total salary of $2,300 for three quarters."

Roland and Willie's only child, Curt Dean, was born later that year, on October 22, 1947. When questioned if his father ever put any pressure on him to become an engineer, Curt responded in the negative. "My grandfather wanted me to be a minister. But my dad told me to make up my own mind on a career. He was supportive of whatever I wanted to do. His big thing was education—to him it was the key to success. So he always encouraged me to get as much education as possible and to be as good as I

---

*Rautenstraus loved giving nicknames to those close to him. Jonathan was the one he gave Buechner.

could at whatever I chose to do. He always liked law and was pretty pleased when I decided to go to law school."

It was in the late 1940s that the young engineering instructor learned first hand about certain peculiarities of Dean Clarence L. Eckel. Raut knew he was firm and strong willed—that Eckel was really the one who hired him as an instructor on his return from the Pacific even though he was to work for Warren Raeder's department. Now Roland found that Eckel truly ran the college with an iron fist. He demanded that his professors put in extra time attending engineering society events. It was an unwritten rule that anyone who didn't make it to Denver for the monthly meetings of the American Society of Civil Engineers need not expect a pay raise next time such came due. So, once a month, the whole crew of civil engineering professors would pile into cars and, as a group, trek to Denver via Arapahoe Road and Highway 287. Many in the department resented these tactics. Rautenstraus just shrugged his shoulders and carried on.

When Roland was appointed, in 1947, to his first national committee for the American Society of Surveying and Mapping—a long list of national engineering committees he would eventually chair—Dean Eckel must have been proud and pleased. So would he be in the years to come, when Rautenstraus became one of the University's most sought-after speakers. In fact, Raut's voracious participation in various conferences reached a fever pitch in later years.

Almost from the beginning of his tenure as an instructor, he assisted Roderic Downing—the perennial conference director—with the Annual Highway Conference staged on campus. In 1958, Rautenstraus took Downing's place as director and held the position until the early 1960s. Prior to that, he would chair and/or be a key speaker at a wide array of conferences, sometimes several in one month.

For example, in 1956: he would chair the session "Impact of the West on the Middle East" at the April 9-12 International Conference on World Affairs; he would address "Civil Engineering Education—What Can We Do About It?" on April 28 at the Annual Meeting of the American Society for Engineering Education; and, a few days later, he would be the keynote speaker at the Annual Conference for Planning Officials stressing the importance of wise land use.

That same summer, Roland would be the director of a special school for the Colorado Department of Highways (now the Colorado Department of Transportation—CDOT), a semester-long instructional program for selected individuals to improve their capabilities as civil engineers. Two summers later, in 1958, he directed a similar program, this time for the purpose of upgrading the skills of CDOT engineers and surveyors for management positions.

The coming years, indeed, found the energetic Roland Rautenstraus engrossed in much more than teaching in college. His national reputation and expertise in land-use planning and transportation, would land him notable speaking engagements at numerous major industry gatherings and conventions. Included was the 1961 National Building Industry Conference where he and well-known developer-builder William Zeckendorf squared-off and laid out their visions for the year 2000. Basically, Zeckendorf saw little reason to restrict growth while Rautenstraus believed in the concept of sustainable development.

In 1949, Rautenstraus—the transfer student from UNC, who was initially reluctant to become an engineer—was awarded his second degree in engineering, a Master of Science in Civil Engineering. President Robert L. Stearns (1939-53), one of the University's longest-reigning leaders, signed both his degrees.

Early in his teaching career, Roland taught students surveying, photogrammetry, geodesy and statics. His class load quickly expanded to include transportation (highway) engineering, city planning, engineering contracts and law, and construction materials, methods and management. Over the course of his career, reported Stein Sture, chair of the department twice (1990-91 and 1994-98), "He taught mostly at the undergraduate level, and usually to large classes." Sture added that Raut "established himself among our best teachers, perhaps, the best instructor of large classes."

His interaction with—and impact on—his students went far beyond the classroom. Bob Adelstein had Rautenstraus as his surveying class instructor in the early 1950s and recalled doing poorly on one of his quizzes. Rautenstraus, who knew Adelstein's father, the founder of Northwestern Engineering, visited with Bob about it. Raut said, "If you're taking engineering because your father wants you to, don't. If it [engineering] isn't fun for you, if it's work, don't do it." (Adelstein—after working for his father's company for a number of years—finally took Rautenstraus' advice and became a psychotherapist, something he enjoys.)

Joe Meheen (BSCE '50) found Rautenstraus to be "imposing, likable and a strict disciplinarian with high standards." He recalled, "One day I walked out of the soils lab and accidentally ran into Raut as he was scolding and berating a hapless student because he had cheated on his exam in some class." Meheen went on to become one of Colorado's leading bridge designers. Steve Holt (BSCE '59), who became one of the state's foremost transportation engineers, had Rautenstraus for construction and engineering law. "Raut was a person you found it easy to connect with, someone who could understand what you were going through. He had a very humorous way of illustrating points so the principles stuck with people forever."

"He brought out the best in people," stated Bob Adelstein's brother Stan (BSCE '53). "He was genuinely interested in people—in how they could make the best of things. He was really fatherly to a lot of us. I'll never forget how he would repeatedly tell us: 'Never look at today for itself. Always look at today as the beginning of something.'"

For someone who had no intention of being a college professor—or even an engineer—Raut got completely wrapped up in it. He no longer talked of traveling the world. He was comfortably settling into university life and putting down roots in Boulder.

In 1954, he became a member of the Boulder City Planning Board, a seat he proudly held for several years. City Manager Don Harmon, who was out of town when Rautenstraus was appointed, wrote him (in a December 21, 1954 letter), "Your reputation is well known, and your accomplishments as well. I look forward with great anticipation to working with you on this very essential service to the citizens of Boulder."

That same year he was promoted to the rank of Associate Professor of Civil Engineering. Ward Darley, the new president of the University (1953-56), signed the official letter confirming his promotion.

Raut passed his state board examinations and became a registered professional engineer (PE) in the state of Colorado in 1955, with license number 1335. (Very few had an earlier and/or longer running registration in the state.) He had already been licensed as a professional land surveyor (PLS). In addition to land surveying, it was now legal for him to practice engineering and seal drawings. Following in the footsteps of his mentor, Eckel, he got involved in doing engineering design work—as well as surveying work—as a consultant, always careful not to alienate engineers in the private sector by competing with them. He did much of his outside engineering work for local consulting engineering companies, including the Ken R.

White Engineering Company, Hartzel Engineering Company and Frank Drexel, Inc.

In 1957, the same year he was appointed to a second City of Boulder board—the Water Board—Rautenstraus was named the youngest full professor on campus. He was just 33. His official promotion came on July 8 with a letter from yet another new CU president, Quigg Newton (1956-63). Raut had only been back on campus for a little over 10 years and his official university papers had been signed by three different presidents. His impression of the position must have been that the life span of the CU presidency was a short and rocky one.

Similar thoughts must have crossed his mind a few years earlier when General Douglas MacArthur—a hero to thousands of American service men like Rautenstraus who served in the Pacific during WWII—was summarily fired by Harry Truman over a disagreement on the Korean War (1950-53). Shortly after the firing on April 15, 1951, Truman signed the Japanese Peace Treaty. It granted Japan full sovereignty, officially ending WWII. The U.S. president's action opened the door for the vanquished country's evolution into one of the world's strongest economic powers. Rautenstraus, curiously, became an advisor to one of its major industries in his later years.

Observing "men of power" such as these must have had some impact on young Roland's outlook, philosophy and plans for the future, as did those of others closer to home. Key engineers around him in the late 1940s and 1950s, who had an influence on his thinking, included the "old men" of the College, Eckel, Raeder and Downing. Their longevity, alone, was amazing. Eckel was at the University so long—nearly 50 years—most thought of him as a CU landmark.

Others with whom Rautenstraus had regular contact and interface included some of the civil engineering department's brightest young faculty members. They included Paul Bartlett (who later became the dean of engineering at CU's Denver campus), William Thoman, Kurt H. Gerstle and Leonard Tulin. "Bill Thoman was one of dad's main mentors," said Curt Rautenstraus. Thoman became nationally known for his work with engineering materials. Gerstle was the recipient of one of the College of Engineering's first two Ph.D. degrees in civil engineering. (He and Jack Hilf received them in 1956.) Gerstle, an internationally known leader in advanced structural theory, ended up spending virtually all of his career at CU.

A colleague of Raut's for 45 years, Leonard Tulin (BSCE '50, MSCE '52), like Rautenstraus, served as chair of the department (1972-76) and spent his entire teaching career at the University. Prior to being hired as an instructor in 1950, he was a student of Raut's. Tulin found him to be "extremely articulate and knowledgeable." Tulin said, "He [Raut] related exceedingly well with his students who were predominately returned veterans, as he was himself. He told it like it was, and he obviously enjoyed being in the classroom. His enthusiasm evoked a similar response from his students."

The enormous influx of engineering candidates in the late 1950s put a tremendous strain on the College of Engineering's facilities and its faculty. The Korean War had ended and many of its returnees came into college on the G.I. Bill. But something else, even greater, drove the unprecedented enthusiasm for engineering. In October 1957, the Russians impressed the world—and shocked Americans—by hurling a satellite into orbit. Overnight, "Sputnik" focused attention on science and engineering, and elevated the status of both. When President John Kennedy issued his challenge to the nation to put a man on the moon by the end of the sixties, there was no shortage of young men and women who took up the call. They rushed off to become engineers.

Exactly one year after Sputnik in October 1958, the University appointed a committee to study the College of Engineering and identify how it could be the leading institution of engineering in the Rocky Mountain region. The committee not only analyzed the college's buildings, which were alarmingly overcrowded, but the overall approach to its future and the mix between research and teaching. Willis Worcester, chair, and Charles A. Hutchinson, vice-chair, coordinated the study. Chairing the subcommittee on "the aims of engineering education" was Roland Rautenstraus.

The committee's final report in September 1959 highlighted three significant recommendations: first, the faculty needed to be strengthened (both in numbers and by professional distinction and national reputation); second, an expanded program of research and graduate study was needed and third, the physical facilities themselves had to be expanded. The study proposed a completely new engineering complex. As reported in *Proud Past...Bright Future*, the committee recommended that "the entire College of Engineering should be moved to the 24th Street and 28th Street area east of the main campus, with a target date of fall 1965 for occupancy of a new complex."

A concept to remodel and expand the college's existing buildings—Hunter, Ketchum, and Engineering I—along "eye-ball alley"* had been suggested prior to the study. The committee, however, completely rejected that proposal as being thoroughly shortsighted, to say the least. And thus began the University's highly ambitious initia-

---

*Eye-ball alley was the wide sidewalk between Ketchum and the two other engineering buildings where the predominately male population of engineering students would lounge, slide-rules hanging from their hips. In the 1950s and early 1960s, they would line up to admire the coeds walking by on their way to and from the women's dorms.

tive to create a modern, new engineering center. It would prove to be a wise and immensely forward-thinking move.

On February 20, 1959, President Newton told Rautenstraus that "you have been appointed Chairman of the Department of Civil Engineering effective July 1, 1959, for a three-year term. For this additional responsibility your total salary will be increased by the amount of $200 a year." One could not get rich advancing up the ladder at CU in those days! Raut had been elected to this position by his peers. "It was the first time the head of the department had been so chosen and named," commented Stein Sture.

To keep the concept of a new engineering complex alive and well, Charles Hutchinson, acting dean after Eckel's retirement in 1960, initiated a committee in October 1961. He selected as its chair one of the most articulate people at the University, Roland Rautenstraus, to "publicize needs for the project to alumni and the people of the State of Colorado," according to *Proud Past...Bright Future*.

The effort proved to be highly effective. The concept of a new engineering center was, in the end, universally well supported. The state legislature passed a bill to authorize it and appropriate its funding. Governor Steve McNichols signed the bill into law in June 1962. The largest construction grant ever made up to that time to the University by the National Science Foundation (NSF)—$1,325,000—helped make the $8.5 million project a reality.

The complex was opened and dedicated four years later (May 5-7, 1966) with much ceremony and fanfare. Several dignitaries were in attendance, including Governor John Love, University President Joseph Smiley, D. D. Smith from the NSF, Dean Max S. Peters, and past Deans Eckel and Hutchinson. The eloquent Roland Rautenstraus would be the master of ceremonies.

On November 17, 1962, both Rautenstraus and Hutchinson, as co-chairs, were appointed to a committee to enlarge the CU engineering program in Denver. This initiative would become a major issue during Rautenstraus' rise to power, and into his presidency.

That same year, the two old comrades shared another collaboration. In December, they received a two-year grant from the Colorado Department of Highways. It required that they head a team of University engineers to do a "two-pronged study leading to improved highways in Colorado." The team was asked to come up with low-cost ways to (1) strengthen paving with chemical and other additives and (2) find ways to prevent roads from crumbling because of swelling soils. Some of the techniques employed by the Seabees on Okinawa came back to Rautenstraus.

Foreign engineers taking a nine-week graduate level course on highway design swarmed the halls of CU's engineering facilities during the summer of 1963. Raul was the director of the program, which was named the Graduate Institute of Foreign Highway Engineers. The Rautenstraus-led initiative was financed by the U.S. Bureau of Public Roads and the International Development Agency, and highway engineers and students from nine countries attended. Much of the material Rautenstraus and Hutchinson developed in their studies for CDOT was presented to the group for the first time.

Then the assassination of President John Kennedy in Dallas on November 22, 1963, sent shock waves around the world. Everyone alive can remember where he or she was that day. The nation mourned JFK and remembered his challenge to put an American on the moon, among other achievements. The effort to fulfill his dream took on new fervor. The University's engineering community and, in particular its aerospace group, became more deeply involved in the national space effort. Kennedy's inspirational words, "Ask not what your country can do for you, but what you can do for your country," were not lost on them.

Men and women such as Rautenstraus never needed much prodding to get involved to make things better. From the JFK assassination on, though, Raut would look at challenges more and more with the eyes of a true citizen of the world.

6

EXTENSION CENTERS
(1964-1969)

C U President Joseph Smiley, with the approval of the Board of Regents, named Rautenstraus associate dean of faculties in May 1964. Raut resigned his position as chair of the Department of Civil and Architectural Engineering shortly after. The first phase of his full-time teaching career ended, though he occasionally taught a class or two over the next 16 years. The year 1964 marked the beginning of a demanding and continuous span in University administration that saw a roller coaster set of events unfold.

Roland's main charge and challenge as associate dean was to coordinate academic planning and development of the Denver and Colorado Springs extension centers. He had taught at the Denver Center every quarter (and every semester once the school went on the semester system) since joining the faculty in 1946 and was familiar with almost every aspect of what this coordination effort required.

Before the mid-1970s, Paul Bartlett recalled, "Students taking classes at the extension centers — whether or not

they took all their classes in Denver or Colorado Springs —
could not get a degree at either place. They had to receive
their degrees on the Boulder campus. In 1972, the state of
Colorado enacted a constitutional amendment approving
the establishment of the University of Colorado at Denver
(UCD) and Colorado Springs (UCCS), giving both the ca-
pability to grant degrees." Bartlett, now dean emeritus of
the UCD College of Engineering, worked closely with
Rautenstraus to bring this about. "My responsibility was
in developing engineering programs at the two places.
Raut," he said, "was responsible for getting all aspects of
the UCD and UCCS operations established. UCCS didn't
have many facilities then and he was very, very instrumental in securing the Cragmor property for the Colorado
Springs campus."

Thurston (Ted) Manning, vice president and dean of
faculty (1964-71), said, "If one person could be said to be responsible for the centers at Denver and Colorado Springs,
it would be Raut." He added, "He was very proud of the
Denver Center — especially the remodeling of the old
Tramway Building, with its two levels of car barns. It was
through his hands-on leadership that the necessary funding
was obtained. During construction, he liked to meet with
the architect, Lamar Kelsey, on a regular basis. They would
get together at the site and walk through the building
checking on its progress. He really loved doing this."

Bartlett's close relationship with Rautenstraus went
back a long way. It began on the Boulder campus in the
late 1940s and fully developed over the years, when, as
Paul noted, "Raut would come down to the Denver campus
before his classes [in the 50s and 60s]. For many years, he
taught both fall and spring terms — and also during the
summer. He was very, very fond of our students on the
Denver campus. I think he really enjoyed them because
most of them were older, more mature, and many times

had jobs and families. He would get acquainted with what they were doing with their potential worlds. They learned a great deal from him, and I truly believe he learned a great deal from them. He was a superlative teacher. I always thought his first love was teaching.

"When he came down early for class, we'd talk about current events, sports and the like. He was just an extremely broad person, interested in most everything. In fact, I can't think of anything he wasn't interested in — that he couldn't make a pretty darned good comment on. I always felt he was highly honest and ethical. He treated everyone — students, colleagues and the public — with great consideration."

Much of what happens in life comes with the "good news" and "bad news" closely linked together. It was no different in Rautenstraus' case. And for him, it started early. When he was five, he began the first grade and within a couple of months the stock market crashed; when he was 12, his sister's wedding was preceded a few months earlier by his older brother's untimely death; when he was completely at ease with his Russell High School classmates and teachers, his family moved before he could finish his senior year.

The year 1964 could be grouped along with these earlier "good-news bad-news" years. Not only was he named, at a relatively young age, an associate dean, but he was also honored, in May, by the College of Engineering with its prestigious Associated Engineering Students Faculty Appreciation Award. It recognized his teaching skills — an honor very meaningful to the teacher in him. It was during this time period that Raut's 76-year-old mother Emma was hospitalized with cancer.

By 1964, the financial fortunes for the Roland Rautenstrauses had taken a solid move upward. They were living well in a nice home in Boulder and Raut was driving a Cadillac. (How he liked those Cadillacs in his middle years!) And he was able to splurge a bit on his wardrobe. He liked nice clothes and had become quite a fashion plate, always with the latest-style sports jacket or suit — neatly pressed. In a Boulder campus student poll, he was one of only a few professors receiving favorable marks for how they dressed. The students said of Raut, "He always looked as if he were going to a dance."

Ted Manning, who was a full dean and ranked above Rautenstraus in the school hierarchy at the time, remembered: "The first time I met Raut was at the airport (Stapleton). He and Willie had come to pick us up in their big Cadillac and take us to a reception at the University. They were dressed to the nines, and looked impressive.

"Raut was a dapper dressing guy. He always wore the latest fashions. I mentioned to him, one time, that my son Peter was going to graduate from junior high and needed a new outfit. Without a blink, Raut volunteered to take him shopping, which he did — to Gano Downs in Denver. They came back with this good-looking outfit highlighted by this first-class, navy-blue blazer — brass buttons and all. My son loved it. But I had to swallow real hard when I got the bill from the store a few weeks later. Raut liked to look good whatever the cost."

"Uncle Rolie," remembered Kent Rautenstraus, "always looked sharp, always had these great-looking — and sometimes wild and colorful — suit jackets and blazers. And it wasn't just his clothes; he always had the latest hairstyle. Even his glasses were what was the rage, fashion-wise."

Manning said, "We became good friends with the Rautenstrauses and did a lot of great things together. Raut and I talked about many things: politics, University issues, sports, history, even technical engineering issues, but we did not talk about personal things." He never discussed his mother, father, brother or sister with Manning, nor how he felt when each died.

Among all his success and accumulation of possessions — and moments of jubilation and satisfaction — an offsetting ledger entry for 1964 was made on July 19. Roland's beloved mother died suddenly. She and Christian, who was 81, were still living in the small, wood-framed house they had custom-built when they returned to Wheat Ridge from his last assignment as pastor of the Lutheran church in Hoisington, Kansas. (The home at 6180 W. 40th Avenue is still in the family. According to their grandson Kent, "four generations of Rautenstrauses have now lived there.")

Curt, who was 16 at the time, recalled his grandmother's funeral as being reverent and serious, and that his father was loving, solemn and dignified. Neither Curt nor his mother Willie remembered that Roland cried. Nor did he shed tears years later when his father and brother passed away. At the funeral of Roland's sister Ruth in the 1980s, though, it was a different story. He was much more shaken and emotional.

In the mid-to-late 1960s, college campuses across the country experienced considerable unrest and dissension, which often resulted in students taking over administrative facilities. The situation at the University of Colorado was no different. Roland told Pam Penfold in 1996 that when CU President Joe Smiley was out of town he was often called upon to protect the president's wife. "Joe traveled a lot and I began to get calls from Mary [Smiley] at 7 or 8 o'clock at night. She would say, 'I'm home alone and there are 500 students outside chanting and I'm scared.' And I would go over to their house." (The president's house was on the Boulder campus at the time. The building is now the Koenig Alumni Center.)

It was then that Rautenstraus, who spent "more than a few nights sleeping on the couch in the Smiley's anteroom," decided that "the president's house shouldn't be so readily available to campus radicals." The Smileys were the last presidential couple to have their home on the CU campus.

During this time, a brash, young graduate student by the name of Paul Danish — who said his life was changed forever by Rautenstraus in the 1970s — led some of the Boulder campus protests. He recalled, "There were a lot of demonstrations beginning to happen [on campus] by 1967 and some of them involved marches on Regent Hall. The administration usually stayed buttoned up in there and sent Raut out to deal with the picketers. We [students] got to know him fairly well through these exchanges. He was in his early 40s then and wore these funny glasses — kind of 'granny glasses' like John Lennon always wore.

"It was clear that here was one guy who really did have a genuine affection for students and was willing to listen. I didn't know his background at the time. He'd just stand there and visit with us with that wonderful little smile he had. I had the feeling watching him that, if I could guess what was going on in his head, it was, to borrow from an old costume melodrama: 'Spoken like a man, but a very young man.' I think that's the way Raut viewed us at the time. And he was right, of course. But he took our ideas seriously and sometimes even acted on them. More importantly, he got us to take some responsibility — come up with solutions, not just complaints."

At the time, Danish was student body vice president (1967-68). He had been editor of the campus newspaper, the *Colorado Daily*, a few years earlier (1963-64) when he was an undergraduate. "One of my most lasting accomplishments then," he said with a grin, "was getting the name of the CU Memorial Center grill renamed the Packer Grill for Alferd Packer [a convicted cannibal in early Colorado history]." Danish later served a term on the Boulder City Council and introduced the city's controversial and nationally discussed anti-growth ordinance of 1976. In 1996, he was elected a Boulder County Commissioner.

Shortly after the Danish-led — as well as other — student "uprisings," Rautenstraus was promoted to vice president for educational and student affairs. On October 18, 1968, a few months after he was named to the position, a reporter from *CU Perspective* interviewed him. Raut outlined some of his beliefs that would affect how he approached his new job, saying, "People should come here [CU] and do the things that motivate them. There should be more student involvement, better facilities, and increased development of the institution so that individuals can develop."

In an earlier interview when he was first selected for the position, he emphasized his background and long history with the University, saying he had "some real feel for the faculty and its relationship to students." He added, "I have always had an abiding interest in achieving the best possible student environment." His comments impressed the reporter who closed the article with, "He [Raut] is possibly the student's best ally in the administration."

One of the first things he did as vice president — with the approval of both Smiley and the regents — was change the duties and titles for the people in charge of dealing with students outside the classroom. He had the traditional titles of dean of men and dean of women abolished. This, he said, was "to be in line with a trend toward less university involvement with students' personal lives. The University should deal with students basically in the context of the learning process. And it doesn't make any difference whether the students are men or women."

To insure these objectives would be accomplished, he appointed James Quigley to the new position of dean of student relations and Pauline Parish as associate dean. The reorganization did not affect two other main areas under his supervision; intercollegiate athletics remained under the direction of Eddie Crowder and alumni affairs stayed under the direction of Dean Graves.

Rautenstraus' new position afforded him the exciting and pleasurable responsibilities of overseeing the school's athletic programs. It presented the old footballer with a chance to, once again, be close to the thrill and action of intercollegiate competition, for women as well as men. And it put him in a position to cultivate relationships with many of the institution's major boosters and contributors — Robert Six of Continental Airlines and Jack Vickers of Vickers Oil, to name two. Both became, in the late 1970s, part of a much hailed plot to hire a big-name football coach. That action would prove to be awkward for Rautenstraus and costly for the University.

On February 11, 1969, Joseph Smiley resigned as the 10th president of the University. It came as a surprise, reported Ronald James in his book *Our Own Generation*, to "most of the campus community and the people of the state, yet it shouldn't have and didn't to those who knew him." Regent Joseph Coors, for one, had lost faith in Smiley and, in October 1968, asked for his resignation — which Coors later withdrew — following events surrounding the national Students for a Democratic Society (SDS) meeting on campus. Rautenstraus, as vice president of student affairs, had not objected to the SDS meeting on campus, even though SDS was well known for its radical ideologies.

Smiley harbored no ill feelings about the matter and, according to James, said, "Raut was certainly a 100-percent loyal supporter of the University. I was pleased to have brought Rautenstraus into the administration in the student affairs area. We got him involved more with alumni and, particularly, in meeting with the legislature, which I felt he did very successfully. There's no question in my mind that Raut is a great friend and supporter of the University . . . highly thought of by the alumni throughout the state and extremely successful in working with the legislature because he's fair, he's down to earth, he doesn't make up things. He just tells it the way it is. He's very effective."

Vice President for Business Affairs Eugene H. Wilson filled in as president after Smiley's departure and until the next president could be hired. Much of the University's business went on at slow speed. The world, though, was abuzz with the landing of Americans on the moon July 20, 1969. Engineer-turned-astronaut Neil Armstrong, after first uttering the words, "That's one small step for man; one giant leap for mankind," planted the U.S. flag on the moon's surface. For many months, Armstrong, an engineer, was the most celebrated man on earth. Another notable engineer — Roland Rautenstraus — was asked to consider the presidency of the University of Colorado. He declined. He was not ready. Yet.

In 1969, Northwestern Construction found itself in serious trouble. The company, which had been in business for nearly 45 years, was being run by the sons of its founder — Stan and Bob Adelstein. The two brothers were not getting along. Company morale and profits were plummeting. And the company's future seemed fuzzy. "We were in great danger of going broke," recalled Stan. A business consultant recommended several corrective measures, such as expanding Northwestern's board of directors to include knowledgeable outsiders.

The consultant specifically suggested one of those board members should come from academia. Almost simultaneously, the brothers thought of one of their old engineering professors — Roland Rautenstraus. Both of them had had him as an instructor when taking surveying and engineering classes at the University of Colorado in the early 1950s. They remembered him as having the vision and leadership skills that could be of tremendous value in their current situation. Over the years, they have given Raut much credit for helping the company survive its crises.

"It was a closely-held company in which I had control," Stan recounted. "My mother held stock until I bought her out in 1970. And Bob had stock until I bought him out along the way. The purchase of his stock was somewhat adversarial — very adversarial, in fact, and Roland acted as a bridge, a real peacemaker.

"He had a real sense of the company's history and what its products were and should be. And he had a great sense of who we were. He had a way of talking to me one way, and would talk to Bob differently. He knew how to address our concerns in a positive way without demeaning Bob or me. I never heard him be mean to anybody in all the time I knew him. He got the two of us to agree to something we could both live with."

Once the sale and buy-out between the brothers were put to rest, they were able to concentrate on the company's future. "Roland told us, 'Try to look downstream.' And that was a key in making our company successful. He had a way about making you see that one of the keys for the future is being able to take a risk not based on the immediate gains of today, or even tomorrow, but on what's going to happen in due time. Roland said, 'Don't worry if you make something that isn't as profitable as you would like today. Look at what's good in the long run.' That philosophy really helped us." Stan continued, "I think that's what he brought to the University. I think he saw the image of CU, not in the time span when he was its vice president and president, but as what he foresaw it would be many years later."

Stan and Bob Adelstein, to this day, remain steadfast in their belief that Rautenstraus — and his insightful advice — fundamentally had much to do, not only with Northwestern's basic survival, but with its great success. "When he came on board, we were doing badly. Our annual volume was only $28 million," recalled Stan. "Roland attended every one of our board of directors' meetings since 1969. During that time, his comments were always tremendously sound, wise and visionary."

Most of Northwestern's meetings were held in South Dakota where the company was based. But, because it was doing quite well in the 1990s, the last one Raut attended (in August 1997) was held in Phoenix. The Adelsteins learned of Roland's death when the company's board packet announcing a record-setting $65 million in billings for the year — along with its invitation to the next meeting in the spring of 1998 — was returned unopened.

For much of 1969, while the University hunted for someone to be its 11th president, Vice President Rautenstraus addressed the issue of *en loco parentis* — a concept literally translated as in place of a parent and characterized by an all-but-defunct idea that universities and colleges should oversee all aspects of students' lives. The concept was nailed in its coffin by the actions of Rautenstraus, who believed CU's students should be treated like adults, not wards of the University. During his term as vice president of student affairs, he systematically eliminated any lingering rules that hindered that concept.

One of the most visible signs of the demise of *en loco parentis* came in August when the Board of Regents abolished the rules prohibiting of-age students from having liquor in their dormitory rooms. "We just felt that students in dorms had the same right that other students had," commented Roland. The sale of 3.2 beer at the University Memorial Center was, likewise, approved. Only Regent Fred Betz voted against the action, with Regent Joseph Coors of Coors Brewery abstaining.

Raut was visibly pleased on August 13, 1969, when he publicly introduced the plans for the construction of CU's new $4 million events building. The institution's expanding sports programs were putting heavy demands on existing facilities. "There is a great need for a building of this nature," Rautentraus told *The Denver Post*. "The largest facility on the campus at the present time is the field house, which was built in 1937. It seats only 4,500 for most events, far below our current needs." One of the new facility's main uses would be for basketball.

Once completed, CU's events building (now called the Coors Events/Conference Center) became the second largest arena in the Big Eight, second only to the one at the University of Kansas. To the 45-year-old engineer, building this facility was a significant University project, one that helped move the institution forward into "the big leagues" of intercollegiate competition. He would learn soon enough if the University's next president held the same view as he did.

The search for the University's new head man was concluded on August 8, 1969, when the regents at a special meeting selected anthropologist Frederick P. Thieme, from the University of Washington, as the person to take the school into the 1970s. His term began the fall semester of 1969. From the day Thieme took over — and until he left — CU's 11th president would put each the Smiley-identified Rautenstraus attributes to the full test.

7

CU BLOOD CELLS
(1970-1975)

"The most serious crisis America has had since the Civil War," declared CU's newly appointed vice president of university relations to a group of CU supporters in Fort Morgan, "is that of the crisis facing higher education." Roland Rautenstraus, who had been named to the new position at the beginning of 1970 by President Thieme, was addressing the group in place of the president.

Thieme promoted Rautenstraus and realigned his administration because, in Thieme's words, "The growth of CU and its expanded academic and research programs has made it essential to divide the academic administration." CU's 11th president named three others to new vice-presidential positions in the shakeup: Thurston Manning (Raut's old boss) for research and planning, James Corbridge for student affairs and Lawrence Silverman for academic affairs. Eugene Wilson, vice president of business affairs, was given the additional duty of secretary for the Board of Regents. (Wilson had been CU's acting president between Smiley and Thieme.)

The excuse given for the appearance by a CU vice president instead of its president that night of May 8, 1970, however, had nothing to do with the restructuring of the administration. Between 8,000 and 10,000 students had assembled on the west side of Norlin Library on the Boulder campus, voted to strike and were threatening to shut down the University. Thieme, a *Fort Morgan Times* article reported, "felt he could not leave the campus because of the situation." The student action was precipitated, according to then student activist David Grimm, by Nixon's invasion of Cambodia. "It really had little to do with dissatisfaction with the University."

The *Times* article reported Rautenstraus told the Morgan County group that the strike was the students' way of showing their concern about the world situation. Their reactions stemmed back to the Vietnam War, the entry of American troops into Cambodia, and the students who died tragically at Kent State.

The Fort Morgan incident was the first of many situations when Roland filled in for Thieme, whose presidency had a short "honeymoon."

The student-unrest portion of Thieme's difficulties extended beyond mere protests. From the late 1960s—the beginning of his term—into the early 1970s, the Boulder campus experienced a series of bombings and episodes of vandalism. The campus ROTC offices were a main target. CU's alumni, the public and legislators were not happy with the situation, to say the least.

"Embattled CU chief fights back—hard" blazed the headline for an October 18, 1970 *Rocky Mountain News* story about the controversial Thieme. The reporter Peter Blake wrote, "At dawn, last Monday, he [Thieme] and Roland C. Rautenstraus, vice president for university relations, piled into a maroon and black Thunderbird and leadfooted it for the Western Slope, there to spend three full days buzzing from civic luncheon to high school to radio interview to reception to alumni dinner to bed and then all over again." Six other CU personnel followed in separate University automobiles.

The tour, which included stops in Delta, Grand Junction, Gunnison and Montrose, was part of an all-out strategy to garner support for the University and put to rest stories that student unrest was destroying the place—and to save Thieme's presidency. Blake reported, "Thieme calls these visits 'total saturation.' His weary aids call it total exhaustion." Two more campaigns had him in Alamosa, Cortez, Durango, Monte Vista, Pueblo, Salida and Walsenburg. "Later this month, he will hit Windsor, Greeley, Sterling and Fort Morgan," stated Blake.

This was an administration with troubles. One of its few bright spots was in an unlikely area: the CU football team had reached national prominence. Athletics were under the direction of Vice President Rautenstraus. He and everyone at the University, especially CU fans across the country, were elated when Colorado defeated Houston 29-17 in the Astro-Bluebonnet Bowl. Their elation soared when, a few days later, the (10-2) 1971 CU team was ranked third in the nation for the season. Any talk of a football dynasty, however, was short lived and would have to wait awhile. (It took CU nearly 20 years to better that national ranking. Colorado, under Coach Bill McCartney, finished No. 1 in 1990 after defeating Notre Dame 10-9 in the Orange Bowl.)

The next year the football team finished 8-4 and, in 1973, it dropped to 5-6. Just as CU's football fortunes continued to slump, so did Thieme's stock in trade. His was still an administration with serious problems. And his troubles did not show any signs of going away, even though the Vietnam War was coming to an end and student unrest was on the decline. When the war's cease-fire agreement was finally signed January 24, 1973, Thieme continued to receive criticism on several fronts. As pointed out by Ronald James in *Our Own Generation*, there was "disturbingly low morale among faculty, students and administrators." One of the few things the administration had to be optimistic about was Rautenstraus' progress addressing the concerns of alumni. Through his efforts, alumni gifts were setting records.

In April 1973, he was called on to do more. The University's first vice president for university relations was also named its first executive vice president. Commenting on the promotion in the *Silver & Gold Record* (April 1973), Thieme said, "I am very pleased to make this announcement. Vice President Rautentraus is eminently knowledgeable and experienced to undertake the duties of executive vice president. He has done an outstanding job and I am sure he will continue to do so in representing the University."

Retaining his duties of coordinating communication between the University and its various publics, Roland took on the additional responsibilities of developing uniform policies and working with the vice presidents overseeing operations, at the four CU campuses. An additional duty was to act in an official capacity for the president in his absence. It was something that "happened a lot in the last year of Thieme's presidency," related John Buechner. "Raut was the University's primary contact with legislators at the time. He was well liked by them, which made him very influential and powerful."

That was why Lanny Pinchuk, from the CU Veteran's Affairs Office, called on Rautenstraus in late 1973. "There was a great deal of unrest at the time because the veterans had been shafted," said Pinchuk. "The state legislature had proposed that young people who were raised in Colorado would no longer be considered residents of the state nor qualify for in-state tuition once they got back from the service—even those drafted for the war in Vietnam—because they hadn't paid state income taxes.

"It was the first time I had met Raut and I was a little nervous," stated Pinchuk. "But he was very relaxed—gracious and magnanimous—and we had a nice conversation. He asked if I could help cool things down and I told him I thought so. He said he would do what he could with the legislature, and he did. I was very impressed with him. He was a distinguished-looking gentleman and was very effusive in his use of the English language." Lanny became the assistant dean of the College of Engineering in the 1980s and had many conversations with Rautenstraus later in that capacity. He said of Raut: "Even if he hadn't been good-looking, he would still impress you because of how he spoke."

In the early 1970s minority groups attending CU were unhappy. They led a series of protests—both on the Boulder campus and at the Denver center—that would result in several unfortunate accidents and fire-bombings. The situations reached such a point of alarm that bulletproof glass was installed in the windows of President Thieme's off-campus house. Police provided protection around-the-clock at his home and at the homes of some of his vice presidents.

The Rautenstrauses were then living in the Frasier Meadows subdivision a couple of miles east of the campus. Willie recalled that "on many occasions, police surrounded our home for protection." One night when Roland was out of town, a group of protesters gathered on their front lawn and demanded Raut appear to discuss matters with them. The police kept in the background, ready to act if required. Willie defused the commotion when she "went out with soft drinks and cookies to talk with them. They were courteous and friendly, and left when it finally sunk in that Raut was really not home. After that, whenever I would go on campus, several of them would call out, 'Hi, Mrs. Rautenstraus,' and come over to visit with me."

As a *Rocky Mountain News* article reported in October 1973 when a handful of Chicano students took over an administrative office in Regent Hall, it was Rautenstraus who brought calm to the situation. Roland led them out of the building to Macky Auditorium so he could address the whole body of protesters—about 200 Chicano and black students. They were demonstrating their concern over the reduction in funding for a minority aid program. Before the uproar was put to rest, State Rep. Sandy Arnold, chair of the Joint Budget Committee, was rushed over from Denver to explain to the crowd why the state had cut the funding. The crowd dispersed when he assured them he would look into reinstatement of the funds.

The promise by Rep. Arnold, however, only pacified the group for a short time. Before the month ended, Governor John Vanderhoof was brought into the melee. A special meeting held in Denver to resolve the grievances of minority students included a full collection of state leaders: the governor, state legislators and top CU administrators. Though many of the pressing issues were resolved at the meeting, the problems did not go away and more serious troubles were to come.

In the spring of 1974, there were more protests on the Boulder campus and several Chicanos were killed in different mishaps. Two incidents vividly stick out in civil engineering professor Stein Sture's memory: the first one at Chautaqua Park south of campus and the second outside the old Pudlick's liquor store on 28th Street. In both incidents, said Sture, "Cars containing three to five Chicanos were blown up." The Boulder police determined the victims were trying to prime or insert blasting caps into explosives and the home-made bombs detonated. Some thought the accidents were planned as part of a conspiracy against minority groups. This proved to be untrue but the issues causing the friction did not get resolved until much later, during the Rautenstraus Administration.

Throughout Raut's time as vice president and president, numerous minority and women students' issues would surface. Most of them were resolved in a win-win way. The reason for Rautenstraus' success in this area was that at his core was a quest for equality and fairness for everyone. In the early 1980s, when David Hays at the Norlin Library Archives was putting Roland's presidential (and vice-presidential) papers in order, Raut told Hays, "Of all the things I did, the one I take the most pride in is opening up the institution to multi-ethnicity." The equal opportunity measures he pushed set him apart from those leaders who came before him. Hays said that many thought three of Rautenstraus' strongest points were student relations, minority relations and his ability to deal with the media, in that order.

By early 1974, the 60-year-old, silver-haired Thieme's stock had sunk as low as it could get. His arrogance in dealing with those outside the University—combined with his poor handling of student unrest and administrative and academic issues—bothered many people. Even his perpetual tan irked some, as did his extravagant ways. In addition to his $50,000 salary (he was the state's highest paid employee in 1974), he had at his disposal a University-owned Thunderbird, a Cadillac and a four-wheel-drive vehicle. He lived in a $100,000 house constructed specifically for him and retained the services of a state-paid cook, housekeeper, gardener and maintenance crew. Changes had to be made and insiders were busy working them out.

By April, rumors predicting President Thieme's final days at CU were flying hot and heavy. The headline for a Pat McGraw story in *The Denver Post* read, "Thieme Rumored to Resign Soon: Rautenstraus Reported Successor."

It only seemed a matter of time, and would he resign or have to be dismissed?

On April 26, 1974, those questions were resolutely answered. By a vote of 7 to 2, the Board of Regents fired the University's 11th president. The vote came immediately after the embattled Thieme read from a prepared statement that ended with: "I do not intend to resign as president of the University of Colorado." Directly after Thieme's removal, the regents named Rautenstraus interim president on a vote of 6 to 3. The three nays were against the appointment only because they thought it might jeopardize Rautenstraus' chances for becoming the permanent president, reported Tom Rees in an April 27 *Rocky Mountain News* story.

An article in the *Silver & Gold* the day of the 11th president's ouster noted that two regents—Dale Atkins and Fred Betz—continued to support Thieme. They felt "he had served in one of the most difficult periods in the history of the University." It further reported, "The period from 1969 to the present has not been a good one for college presidents. While no one has studied the turnover rate at major institutions, it would be safe to estimate that an impressive percentage of those who held presidencies in the fall of 1969 are no longer at their jobs."

In these turbulent and troubling times CU needed strong, solid leadership—someone like Roland Rautenstraus. He knew the University and those closely involved with it better than any man alive. "If anyone could control the chaos, it was Raut. He not only clearly understood the workings of the University, but was someone who had institutional loyalty," confirmed Regent Jack Anderson. His predecessor (Thieme) later said of Rautenstraus, "If you took a sample of blood, his cells would have CU on them. If I would have had the knowledge that Raut has when I came here—to know where all the bodies were buried and so on—I would have been able to handle things quite a bit better."

How different Raut was from Frederick Thieme. As a long-time moderate Republican with liberal leanings—liberal on social issues but financially conservative—he insisted on remaining in the home where he then lived to save the University the expense of owning a president's house. He still liked Cadillacs, but would do with one car rather than the three Thieme had. David Grimm, who became Rautenstraus' special assistant after his installation as permanent president, recalled that, when the regents asked him if he wanted the standard contract, Raut said, "I don't need a contract. You just tell me when it's time to step down." He would *not* need to be fired.

The *Colorado Daily*, a few days after Roland's appointment, reported, "Rautenstraus looks and acts much like the model of a college president. He is calm, dapper, straightforward and gentlemanly. He speaks three languages fluently, has an envious teaching record and is widely respected in his field of civil engineering." The article's author, Brian Waidmann, additionally pointed out, "By his count, he has held 20 jobs within the University, running the gamut from assistant instructor to president. 'I can honestly say that there has not been one job here that I didn't find to be a lot of fun.' For more than 30 of his 50 years, the University has been his life, home and, he insists, his church. He firmly believes that higher education and the University can only improve society. That is the crux of his religion."

"This university is my church as much as my father [a Lutheran minister] had his," said Raut. His nephew Kent Rautenstraus recalled that statements like that did not set well with his grandfather Christian nor with older members of the family who, unlike Roland, continued to be regular and devout churchgoers. "Everyone in the family was very proud of uncle Rolie and what he had accomplished," stated Larry Dumler. They were not, however, pleased about his seemingly irreverent attitude toward organized religion.

In May of 1974 Rautenstraus was honored by the CU Alumni Association with its highest alumni honor, the Norlin Medal, for outstanding accomplishments in one's chosen field. His citation recognized him not only for moving through the academic ranks at CU—from instructor to interim president—but also for his accomplishments as an engineer and his contributions to the community-at-large. Also highlighted were his contributions to the development and growth of the campuses at Denver and Colorado Springs, and his important role as legislative liaison with the state General Assembly and the governor on behalf of the University.

The list of Rautenstraus' endorsers of his nomination for the Norlin Medal read like a virtual "Who's Who" of Colorado politics and higher education. It included Governors John Love and John Vanderhoof, CU presidents Joseph Smiley, William Baughn, Eugene Wilson and Fred Thieme, and Thurston Manning, then president of the University of Bridgeport in Connecticut.

Earlier, the Alumni Association had honored Rautenstraus with its other top award, the prestigious Robert Stearns Award, a recognition for outstanding service to CU. The Norlin and Stearns awards were named after and inspired by two of the institution's longest reigning and most admired presidents—George Norlin (1919-39) and Robert Stearns (1939-53). President Stearns had signed both of Roland's CU diplomas. (Rautenstraus is the only person ever to receive both the Norlin Medal and Stearns Award.)

Rautenstraus exhibited his quick wit in front of thousands at CU's 1974 May commencement. As had become the custom because of the large number of spring graduates, the ceremonies were held in Folsom Stadium. During the festivities, while the new interim president was handing out diplomas, one of the male graduates felt the urge to slip off his clothes and run up on stage, kiss a female receiving her diploma on the cheek, then streak naked out of the arena with the campus police in pursuit. Dennis Weingardt (BSCE '74) who received his engineering degree that day, said, "Everyone was stunned and in shock. It was a tense situation but Rautenstraus took it in stride and put the crowd at ease by remarking, 'As you can see, we have some healthy students.' He got a laugh and put everyone at ease. I'll always remember how well he did that."

Even though University matters now demanded most of his time, Roland did not ignore broad societal issues. Long a spokesman and crusader for sound community planning, efficient transportation design and the wise use of natural resources—especially energy, Rautenstraus was involved with a number of policy-setting boards. His service on one of them, Colorado's Energy Task Force, began May 24, 1973, when he was appointed to its executive committee by Governor John A. Love. Shortly after he placed Roland on the Task Force, Love was named by President Richard Nixon as the nation's energy czar. It was a brief appointment.

The Watergate scandal brought President Nixon down on August 9, 1974, and moved Gerald Ford—someone quite familiar with Colorado—into the White House. The Fords, like Roland and Willie, had long owned a home in Vail. In 1976, Betty Ford would stay with the Rautenstrauses in Boulder. "The Secret Service precautions around our house were unbelievable," remembered Willie. She was especially irked when Secret Service agents carelessly trampled on her beloved roses while being protective of Mrs. Ford. It was even more of a nightmare when Raut took the First Lady to the October 9 Colorado-Nebraska football game, which, to Raut's dismay, CU lost 24-12.

The selection process to find a permanent replacement to fill the CU presidency continued to plod along throughout 1974. The nationwide search had uncovered more than 300 candidates and the selection committee—made up of mostly academicians—had its hands full. The students always supported Rautenstraus; his endorsement from the faculty, though, was not that certain. Many outside the University wondered why he was not named its permanent president from day one. They clamored for a decision sooner rather than later.

An article in the *Daily Camera* on December 19, 1974 was headlined, "Rautenstraus Students' Choice For CU President." It reported that students from Boulder, Denver and Colorado Springs had made their choice and it was Roland Rautenstraus. The article stated that students were convinced Raut had "proven his ability to the state legislature and the citizens of Colorado. In addition to having a wealth of experience and clear dedication to the task of administering the University, we believe Mr. Rautenstraus has performed the job of University [interim] president in an exemplary fashion."

The group that Raut most believed a university should exist for showed they wanted him. It must have delighted him to have the students' approval and endorsement. But what was going on in the minds of the people on the two bodies—the selection committee and the Board of Regents—that would control the final decision?

8

TWELFTH PRESIDENT
(1975-1976)

Finally, it was made official on January 14, 1975. The University of Colorado Board of Regents unanimously voted to continue Roland C. Rautenstraus as the 12th president of the University. The 50-year-old Rautenstraus, who had been serving as interim president since April 26, 1974, was entrusted with preparing the institution for its second century and moving it forward to greatness. At the same time, it was hoped he could put a stop to the turmoil and disruption the institution had been experiencing over the previous 10 years. Many had extremely high hopes he would be the right man at the right time. "Rautenstraus is the man for the University right now," proclaimed Regent Eric Schmidt.

Byron Johnson, a 12-year regent, also pointed out that Rautenstraus had "very strong support from all sides: alumni, public officials, administration, students and faculty." Regent Jim Carrigan emphasized, "One of the things very influential to me [in selecting Raut] was the position of the students at the Boulder campus." They boycotted the official search committee because of a lack of adequate student representation and over-representation of faculty.

The students formed their own committee and turned in the name of Rautenstraus as their one and only nominee for the position.

There had been other highly qualified candidates under consideration for the position, so it was a substantial feather in Rautenstrus' cap to have received such high and enthusiastic endorsement from the regents, students and the community-at-large. Besides Rautenstraus, the other top finalists ready to accept the job—according to Frank Barnes, chair of the selection committee—were Donald Kennedy and Paul Gray. (Kennedy went on to become president of Stanford University and Gray became president of Massachusetts Institute of Technology).

Definitely tilting the scale in Raut's favor was the fact that the regents wanted someone who knew how the place worked and could bring some order. Rautenstraus fit the bill on both counts. Regent Richard Bernick said, "Raut was our first choice and was elected on the first ballot." He added that Rautenstraus, with his "very relaxed attitude," always had a calming effect. And he was admired for getting "people to work together for higher purpose. He had this very special quality for being persuasive but not abrasive."

Regent Jack Kent Anderson, who nominated Roland for the position, had previously been chair of the Alumni Association and knew how highly Raut was thought of by the alumni. Regent Geraldine Bean seconded the nomination by saying Rautenstraus had been "doing a good job of administering the University" as interim president and had "mended a lot of hard feelings which existed between the faculty and administration." In summing up Roland's abilities, Anderson said, "Raut will bring calm to a chaotic situation." It was a situation created, to some extent, by the composition of the board itself and the characters of the individual regents—past and present.

It became evident in the early 1970s that the board's make-up needed to be altered. Back in 1970, Regent Joseph Coors, a Republican, made it known publicly that if the two Democratic incumbents—Regents Betz and Johnson—could be defeated and replaced by their Republican challengers then-President Thieme's job would be in jeopardy. All six seats on the then-six-member CU board would be held by one political party. Betz and Johnson, however, prevailed and Thieme's presidency was saved, at least until 1973. Even though, on paper, CU presidents do not get involved in partisan politicking, the Coors' threat, to a large extent, was the reason for the whirlwind Thieme campaigns made in the fall of 1970.

Shortly after that year's shenanigans, the structure of the Board of Regents was changed from six members to nine, saving the president from having the untenable position of deciding tie votes. To fill the positions until the next election, Governor John Love (a Republican) appointed the three new members—two Republicans and a Democrat, one banker and two lawyers—producing a board with six Republicans and three Democrats.

The governance and administration of the University are allegedly non-partisan. However, the reality was—and is—different. The Coors-led situation in 1970 was a good illustration. The constantly changing balance of political persuasions of a micro-managing group of regents in the early-to-mid-1970s affected, as much as anything, where the University was heading in the latter part of the 70s. What were the challenges facing the 12th president of CU and who were his bosses?

In 1974, while Rautenstraus was executive vice president, the board consisted of five Republicans and four Democrats. One year later, when he started his presidency, it consisted of six Democrats and three Republicans.

A *Colorado Daily* article (January 20, 1975) reported, "Rautenstraus, whose strong GOP ties are well-known, is not disturbed that many Colorado legislators [and regents] are Democrats. 'I have dealt with the legislature in a bi-partisan manner. I am only partisan toward the University,' he said. Working with the legislature for University funding will take up much of his time for the next few months."

The story's reporter, Keith Sealing, also pointed out, "Rautenstraus has a theory that university presidents are picked based on their ability to solve the problems of the day. The most pressing one is answering the question, how do you make the institution significantly better at a time of relatively strong financial constraints?" Rautenstraus was confident he could work equally well with regents of either party, that their—his and the regents—battle would be with the state legislature, not each other. Time proved this to be true.

The second part of Sealing's question was how Raut could "maintain a sincere dedication toward higher education when it seems to be popular to be critical and negative, when the mood of society is negative?" Raut felt it would take the full and cooperative efforts of many: the administration, faculty, students, alumni, legislators and the public—and especially the regents. "The University is a great place and all of us working together can make it even greater."

Supportive leadership from the regents would certainly be needed and advantageous. Those who could assist the new president immensely included old and new members. The only two regents who were around when Rautenstraus was named executive vice president and president—and were present at his resignation—were Anderson, a lawyer, and Johnson, an economics professor and long-time state legislator. Both of them—one a Republican and the other a Democrat—became key to Rautenstraus' performance.

Four other regents spent nearly as much time with him: Geraldine Bean, Fred Betz, Sr., Thomas S. Moon and Eric W. Schmidt. They were in office both at the time Raut was named executive vice president and then president— but would not be around when he left office. Of the three new members on the board that selected Rautenstraus— Louis F. Bein, Richard J. Bernick and Jim R. Carrigan—only Carrigan would not be around when he stepped down. When CU's 12th president left office in January 1980, the Board of Regents included: Anderson, Bein, Bernick, Fred Betz, Jr., Peter Dietze, Johnson, Sandy Kraemer, Rachel Noel and David Sunderland. Each and every one of them had an impact on the Rautenstraus and his presidency.

To fulfill the vision for CU's future greatness, Raut and the regents knew that the instituion would need more and more state funding. Keeping and improving strong relations with the state legislature was crucial and Roland was encouraged to do just that. Concerning the dollar amounts, Rautenstraus stated (in a *Rocky Mountain News* article by Tom Rees on January 19, 1975), "The University is seeking more than $124 million for all four campuses in 1975-76. That would be up from about $101 million this year."

"Rautenstraus," the *News* article also reported, "said he proposes to ask the state to consider sponsoring more research, 'particularly in areas that are important to the residents of the state.' Such research, he suggested, could provide information for the legislature and the executive branch to use in making policy decisions."

In addition to funding, the other major priority facing the Rautenstraus administration, from day one, was—as reported by Rees—completing "the University's reorganization into four 'fairly autonomous' campuses along the Front Range of the Rockies." At the time Rautenstraus became president, the University had a total of 34,000 students—21,000 of them on the Boulder campus with the rest at CU Denver and Colorado Springs, and the CU Health Sciences Center in Denver. The regents, in adopting the CU reorganization plan, created the position of chancellor—as the chief administrative officer of each campus—reporting directly to the president. A pressing chore for President Rautenstraus in early 1975 was to select chancellors for both the CU Health Sciences Center and the Boulder campus.

The regents and state legislators must have been pleased to read in the same *News* article that, even with the reorganization, the University's 12th president was "going to run a more Spartan administration, one that's consistent with cost containment." He promised, "I'll be reducing rather than increasing administrative costs."

Asked by Pat McGraw of *The Denver Post* (January 19, 1975) how long he thought he would last as president, Raut responded, "I hope not one day longer than the time I'm reasonably effective. Some of the greatest tragedies I've seen involved people who stayed on after they had lost their effectiveness." He also stated that three significant issues he was eager to address as president were: "(1) How do you improve the basic instructional program of the institution—and how do you make the learning experience the most exciting time possible? (2) With the federal funding dropping off, how do you develop other [funding] areas? (3) How do you get Colorado leaders to support research?" He stressed, "We need to make the University increasingly useful to the state."

Because they wanted to remain in their own home during his term, Raut and Willie had to build an addition. Their son Curt, a graduate of the CU law school, lived on his own and practiced law in Louisville, Colorado. Hence, they had enough bedrooms. But they did not have enough space to do the kind of entertaining presidents and first ladies must do. So, early in his administration, the Rautenstrauses lived through the trials and tribulations of a significant home-improvement project while still adjusting to his new duties. Once the project was completed, CU's president and first lady frequently entertained a wide cross-section of people. Guests in their home ranged in rank from First Lady Betty Ford to student groups. Whatever the size of the event—large or small—Willie Rautenstraus soon established a reputation as one of Colorado's stellar hostesses.

To add to the commotion of living in a house during renovations, Raut also took on the task of moving his office out of Regent Hall to a smaller building at 914 Broadway. A picturesque Gothic structure, the building had once been the Pi Kappa Alpha Fraternity house. The Regent Hall space was taken over by the Boulder campus administration and its acting chancellor, Lawson Crowe. The office for the regents also stayed in Regent Hall. The Pi Kappa Alpha building was renamed University Hall and became the headquarters for University-wide operations—and the office of the president—from that time forward.

Raut liked the new arrangement and space, especially his personal office. It was quite spacious with a large wood-burning fireplace. On one side, near the fireplace, was his desk and across from it a couple of sofas. On the other side of the room was a large and impressive solid-wood conference table for larger meetings. Rautenstraus, who appreciated a wide range of music from classical to jazz and even some country and western songs, had a quality stereo sound system installed immediately. David Grimm said he would often encounter Raut working alone on Saturdays, his fireplace roaring and stereo at full volume. Frank Sinatra or other favorite singers crooned away while he worked on school matters.

When he delved into difficult budget issues, however, Rautenstraus turned to classical music. During an interview in January 1977, he told Edward Murray of the *Daily Camera*, "There's nothing I like better on a cold winter afternoon than to come up here [his University office], get a good fire going, put some Wagner on the hi-fi, and then settle down to cut budgets."

Rautenstraus hired John Buechner as CU's first director of public affairs to handle daily legislative relations for him since his presidential duties did not allow him enough time to do it any longer. John recalled the many long hours they spent working in front of the fireplace. When Buechner was first picked for the position, he told Roland, "I'm going to do the best job I can for you and you have my complete loyalty. And he replied, 'Jonathan, the only loyalty I want you to have is to the University of Colorado.' I think he said that over and over to a lot of people.

"Raut was extremely articulate, with an astonishing vocabulary. His voice was very powerful and he had a mellifluous way of delivering words. I went into his office one time and asked, 'How are things going?' and he answered, 'They're going singularly sanguine.' He used alliteration all the time. One time he was at his desk with his head in his hands when I came in. He told me, 'Right now I'm thinking something through because a reporter wants to ask me a question and I want to make absolutely sure I know how to respond to it.' I think that was the first time I realized it just didn't come off the top of his head—that he carefully weighed his words. He was not a hip-shooter. He gave the impression at times that it was very easy and familiar to him—that he could address any topic. That was when I realized that, when you're head man, you do weigh your words carefully."

Prior to becoming full president—when he was still interim president—Rautenstraus described the position to the *Coloradan* (Vol. 77, 1975) as "more of a way of life than a job." His schedule, he told the editor, often entailed 15-hour days attending to presidential functions. "Meetings and social functions consume much of his time. For home football games he entertains 100 to 200 guests. He says he's lucky if he goes home before 10 p.m. on weekdays. He especially enjoys talking to students to find out what they think on most anything. An occasional stroll through campus at midday or a dinner in a dorm are two ways he establishes student contact."

"Spending time in the dorms and with the outside public," Raut went on record as saying, "is essential for effective decision making. You can't anticipate making reasonable decisions if you don't have a feel for what people want. You've got to keep trying to get in other people's positions. It's the only way I know how to operate."

Rautenstraus admitted the powers of the presidency were awesome, saying, "It's a tremendous ego-reinforcing world. I have thousands of former students all over the country. It's hard to go places without seeing students who have known me."

Because the position required considerable traveling within tight time constraints, he had to overcome his 30-year-old flying phobia, as well as his claustrophobia. He had no choice. The use of air travel was the only way he could fit in all the meetings he had to attend.

Concerning leisure activities, he said, "I play tennis every now and then. I play it badly but I hack away at it. But the University is my favorite leisure. I guess it would be after spending almost 30 years here."

Buechner, one of Raut's regular tennis playing pals, remembered him not as a "hacker" but as a "very aggressive player. We played almost every week—at 10 p.m., at the old Boulder Tennis Center—and Raut was very competitive. So was Curt (Roland's son), who was also one of our regulars." Curt admitted, "My dad was sort of the

'Shannon Sharpe'* of the tennis court." The other member of the fearsome foursome tennis group was architect Dwayne Nuzum, a long-time friend and contemporary of Rautenstraus. Nuzum became the executive director of the Colorado Commission on Higher Education in the 1990s.

Shortly after the end of his first year, CU's 12th president delivered one of his oratorical masterpieces at the summer commencement exercises in his unique voice and style. It took place on a beautiful, sunny summer day—August 16, 1975—with flags and banners flapping in the breeze, and the band playing off-and-on throughout the activities.

As one of the highlights of the ceremonies, the University received the official Bicentennial flag. Regent Bean, in accepting the flag and recognition of CU as a "Bicentennial University," agreed it would offer programs that would carry out the Bicentennial themes of "Heritage, Festival and Horizons" with lasting significance.

In his address, President Rautenstraus used the occasion of the country's upcoming bicentennial and the school's centennial to urge the graduates to make their own history. "These are still times trying souls," he claimed, "As in 1776 and 1876, there are still great things yet to do. May I suggest only that you try your souls first with a manageable mission. Don't feel personally obligated, as graduates of the University or as human beings, to necessarily have to be a drummer in the next American revolution, to win a Nobel prize or to write the Great American Novel. Begin as individuals with a modest prospectus.

"As Socrates urged, get to know and put up with yourselves a little better ... before you set out to explain that a

---

*The wise-cracking NFL all-pro tight-end for the Denver Bronco football team, known for taunting opposing players.

graduate may decide, for example, to become a general practitioner in a rural community rather than doing research in a large urban hospital. You can't ignore nor should you try to insulate yourselves from the big issues of the times. That is not possible if you value sanity, and if you hold the value of commitment.

"But don't hitch your wagon to a falling star. Keep it on the ground and, to mix metaphors, brighten the corner where you are. Then, if your light comes to illuminate a larger landscape in time, so much the better. Whatever it is you have inherited of good and evil from the world you never made, the earth is really now yours to reshape, and reshape you can if you have the will.

"The last quarter of the 20th century is yours; and you will have a portion of the 21st century to leave in better shape for those who come later. Keep your mission manageable and you will be surprised how much you will accomplish."

On November 1, 1975, Raut was reunited with an unlikely character from his past —colorful Fritz Brennecke, one of the head coaches for the state's first high school all-star football game in which Raut played (in 1942). The two were honored by the University of Northern Colorado (UNC) for their many contributions to Colorado, and received the school's two most prestigious awards for such. Brennecke, director of athletics and physical education at Colorado School of Mines, was honored with the Trail Blazer Award "for his great efforts on behalf of intercollegiate athletics." Rautenstraus was presented with UNC's first-ever Columbine Award for his "outstanding contributions to business, engineering and education."

Both lived in Colorado and knew of each others' accomplishments but neither had spoken to the other since the 1942 football game. Fritz and Raut were known as good storytellers and they must have entertained the crowd with their lively renditions of their team's stirring 3-0 victory against all odds. The *Greeley Tribune* story on the gala event did not mention whether either of the two award recipients believed the win on the gridiron 33 years earlier was the result of stellar coaching or athletic performance.

From the latter part of 1975 to January 1976, President Rautenstraus was deeply involved in negotiations to hire the first permanent chancellor for the Boulder campus—replacing interim Chancellor Lawson Crowe. Raut wanted to open the University to multi-ethnicity and his selection would do that. It would, however, prove to be unfortunate as well as history-making. But it showed where CU's 12th president was coming from and what he wanted to accomplish during his reign.

9

JOURNEY TO AFRICA
(1976-1978)

On January 23, 1976, the regents accepted a recommendation from Rautenstraus to hire Mary Berry from the University of Maryland not only as CU's first female chancellor at the Boulder campus but as CU's first black chancellor. Berry, a provost of behavioral and social science at the College Park campus of Maryland and a member of the Washington, DC Bar Association, was a specialist in American constitutional, legal and Afro-American history. Her term in office in Boulder, which officially began July 1, ended almost before it began.

Shortly after Berry was named chancellor, President Jimmy Carter appointed her assistant secretary for education in the U.S. Department of Health, Education and Welfare (HEW). She requested and received from Rautenstraus a one-year leave of absence. This dismayed CU faculty members at Boulder who expressed concern about the problems that would be caused by the chancellor being gone for a year. Then a bombshell dropped on Raut and the regents. A *Denver Post* story quoted Berry as stating, during the Senate hearing confirming her Carter appointment, that she would remain with HEW for four to eight years.

Much consternation, uncertainty, claims and denials ensued for months until, in May 1977, it was all put to rest. Berry agreed to resign as CU's chancellor. In her resignation letter to Rautenstraus, she stated, "The allegations of conflict of responsibilities and dual salaries are utterly false. However, those allegations have resulted in rumors of reprisals against the University as well as tensions within my Washington office. I find this an untenable position." Raut's long-time colleague Jim Corbridge assumed Berry's duties while the search for her replacement proceeded.

Catching Rautenstraus before he left for a February 1976 road trip to Lamar in southeastern Colorado, Lynne Domash of the *Colorado Daily* got him to talk about his typical day. (He had been in office for a year-and-a half.) Rautenstraus first briefed Domash on his trip to Lamar saying he was meeting with public officials, prospective donors and officials from state institutions—and with Regent Fred Betz, editor of the local newspaper.

Domash reported, "It's 8:30 in the morning and he's already behind schedule. As usual, the unexpected has come along to play havoc with what started as a carefully planned day. Between phone calls from legislators, administrators and faculty members, he's seen a group of angry faculty members protesting certain actions by the administration [the Berry issue?]." Eventually there came a break and he visited with Lynne.

"I'm a captive of the people," Rautenstraus told the reporter. He relaxed in an easy chair and lit a cigarette. "I decide how to spend the day, but I'm thwarted by circumstances. An atypical day is a typical day here. The day starts early and runs late—but then so do most other people's in the University. The days are long and you do work weekends. You represent the University to the people of the state, and play a major role in generating resources for the institution.

"And you work with the governor, the legislature, donors, agencies who support research; meet with the students, the faculty, staff and administrators, and the Board of Regents. And you have to do a lot of traveling. I spent Thursday and Friday in Washington, DC, meeting with different agencies who support the University." To help deal with his dislike for flying—and pass the time on his cross-country trips—he often did crossword puzzles. Word games were a life-long passion of his.

Domash, who referred to Rautenstraus as "charming" and having a "winning smile," felt he was "always the diplomat," carefully avoiding taking credit for certain things the University accomplished since he took office. Raut continued to be a sought-after speaker. What was not mentioned during the interview was his upcoming trip to Africa funded by the State Department and American Council of Education. It would become intellectual ammunition for many of his future speeches.

Sometime in March 1977 Rautenstraus did what lesser men would not even consider. He hired a liberal environmentalist to be his special secretary and speech writer. Not only that, Paul Danish came with the label of being one of those campus trouble-makers spearheading the student demonstrations of the late 1960s. Though he had political leanings more in tune with the Republican Party, Raut put them aside and brought Danish on board because he admired Paul's thinking and many of his visionary ideas.

Since Danish's departure from CU in 1968, Raut's new speech writer had worked for some notable newspapers—the *San Francisco Chronicle*, the *Detroit Free Press* and Boulder's *Town and Country Review*—and several of his writings had captured Rautentraus' attention. From May 1971 to October 1972, Danish had been in Israel writing grant proposals for the Institute of Arid Zone Research, which helped establish him as a journalist with a broad perspective of the emerging world situation. In a way, he served as Rautenstraus' "devil's advocate" on certain hotly debated issues. Plus, he was a good writer who quickly got in tune with the message—and personal style of delivery—Raut wanted to communicate.

Rautenstraus, the master orator, taught Danish that speeches should "tell people the importance of what they're doing and bring out the higher good in people— bring out the best in people." In Paul's mind, "The keynote address he [Raut] gave at the national convention of Agronomists in Fort Collins shortly after his trip to Africa [in the fall of 1977] was a defining speech." It forever remained one of Raut's favorite speeches because he felt it clearly illustrated "how important it is to hear from within oneself," a solemn tenet of his. (The speech is reprinted in Appendix B.)

To Danish, "Roland represented what was best of his generation—a true child of the century. He bridged the cultures identified in Snow's provocative 1956 essay, 'Two Cultures,' which deals with the conflict between the scientific intellectuals (engineers, etc., who make the world work) and the literary intellectuals (lawyers, etc., who run it)."

"I'm delighted that you will be able to be with us at Commencement in May to accept the honorary doctor of laws degree from the University of New Mexico," wrote William (Bud) Davis, president of UNM, in a March 15, 1976 letter to Rautenstraus. In addition to Raut, another notable would be honored at the same time for his work on subjects near and dear to Roland—literature and western history. Robert M. Utley, a noted western historian and author of several books on the west, would receive an honorary doctor of letters degree. Utley was the assistant director of the National Park Service. The two of them struck up a lasting relationship because of Roland's ever-increasing concern about the country's natural resources.

Curt Rautenstraus said his father was so proud of this honorary law degree that "I always thought he would have loved being a lawyer." Raut taught engineering contracts and law at CU for years and often chided Curt, a practicing lawyer, that he was going to join his firm as a partner now that he had a law degree from UNM, and take on the more difficult cases. "My dad was like that. He liked to bait people, needle them. He was not a big joke teller, but he did enjoy teasing, giving everyone a nickname and playing practical jokes." His teasing and punmaking began early. Gloria (Dole) Nelson—Sen. Bob Dole's sister—recalled that her brother and Roland "used to compete with their puns (to see who could outdo whom)," back in their Russell days.

"My dad had this fantastic memory," said Curt. "He could remember details from way back in his youth: stories, anecdotes, songs, poems and even passages from the Bible. And he would use them when he ribbed people." His wit many times included the use of limericks. One of his favorite limericks he would often fit into a teasing situation was by Ogden Nash: "A primal termite knocked on wood. And tasted it and found it good. And that is why my sister May . . . fell through the floor today."

Rautenstraus was so sure of himself, he never had trouble with self-effacement. He was, from the early 1950s, an extremely busy speaker at any number of events. Often his speeches—like the one in front of a large group of intellectuals from around the world at the Vail Symposium on August 11, 1977—began with: "Sometimes one gets admonitions from all quarters. I was told that I would be in no jeopardy if I didn't talk longer than five minutes. My father, who was a theologian, told me from the time I was just a boy to be either brilliant or brief, and since he never gave me the endowment for the former, I've made the latter a practice."

During the spring, summer and fall of 1976, a goodly amount of Rautenstraus' time—and that of other CU administrators and staff—was spent preparing for the college's up-coming 100-year celebration. Old Main, the first (and only) building on campus in 1876-77 was being renovated. They scheduled kick-off celebrations for September 7, the day the first class of 44 students entered Old Main in 1877. According to early newspaper accounts, CU's first president Joseph Sewall spent most of his time that day just worrying and nervously pacing the floor wondering if there really would be a university.

Eugene Wilson, president emeritus and chairman of the University's Centennial Commission, pointed out that, in the beginning, the college only had a couple of professors. "The original 44 students were taught by President Sewall and one other faculty member. Today, there are about 21,800 students, 2,000 faculty and 4,000 staff (on the Boulder campus)." There were budget and funding problems back in 1876, but the numbers were minuscule compared to those in the late 1970s.

"Regents Ask Record Budget Of $162 Million for 1977-78" ran the headline in *The Denver Post* feature story for August 20, 1976. The seemingly never-ending financial appetite of the state's largest and most prestigious educational institution did not go unnoticed by the state legislature. Some were of the opinion CU was getting too pretentious—"snooty"—and too big for its own good.

A movement was underway in 1976 that would eventually cause Rautenstraus to rethink his future. It would severely shake up the University's leadership and faculty. A firmly capped enrollment and curtailed state funding were its main ingredients. By doing this, legislators hoped it would encourage large numbers of would-be college students (from Colorado) to attend smaller colleges spread around the state. The movement would continue until the end of the decade, and beyond.

In November 1977, Roland made a journey to Africa. As viewed by Paul Danish (Raut's speech writer and devil's advocate), it was a life-defining moment for Rautenstraus, a true eye-opener for him. It seemed to be the catalyst that gave him a deeper and more intimate sense of the plight of Third World—emerging—countries and the changing world order. When he did consulting work for companies from industrial nations in the 1980s and 1990s, he was often reminded of what he learned on that excursion. It was his first significant foray abroad since his days in the Pacific during WWII.

Like Abraham Lincoln, also an infrequent church-goer, Rautenstraus—according to his son Curt—always believed in a higher being. Otherwise, as he told Curt, "how could one find the meaning of life?" He had to weave into that search how people from emerging and industrial countries fit together in the puzzle. It was ironic that the place where Christian Rautenstraus, as a young man, dreamed of being a missionary—Africa—would have such a major impact on his youngest son. As with Africa, future trips to South America and small countries like Puerto Rico and Haiti also had a lasting effect on Raut.

The five African countries Roland visited in 1977 with other university presidents selected by the State Department were Egypt, Kenya, Nigeria, Sudan and Zambia. Rautenstraus often traveled and roomed with Samuel Cook, president of Dillard College, a predominately black institution in New Orleans. The touring American educators were particularly interested in the applicability of various educational systems and technology transfer. The State Department wanted the university presidents' recommendations for U.S. policy on education in the international arena.

In an article in the *Silver & Gold Record* (December 13, 1977), Rautenstraus wrote, "I think the thing that impressed me most [about Africa] was that in every country we visited, the government officials and other notables we met were unanimous in their desire to obtain the technology—and more nearly the mode and quality of life—that we have in the United States. They want the technology; they want the housing; they want the health care; they want the goods the average American takes as the natural order of things. And it is to that end that every one of these countries without exception is markedly expanding its educational programs at the university level, under the expectation and the belief that this will make a more profound change in the lifestyles of those countries than any other single thing that they are able to do."

Drawing a parallel with development in the United States, Rautentraus identified another major and unique ingredient in America's story of unmatched economic success, saying, "American industry had available to it a pool of scientists, engineers—and perhaps equally importantly, technicians, mechanics and machinists—that made possible the swift development, utilization and commercialization of the scientific and technical discoveries of the day. It is hardly accidental that many innovations that were European in origin remained laboratory curiosities until America got hold of them."

During 1978, the CU administration and the state legislature held constant discussions back and forth, dealing with the University's enrollment and budget. Even though much of the daily contact with legislators now belonged to John Buechner, Rautenstraus' director of public affairs, Raut, as CU's president, stayed involved. When Roland did similar assignments for President Thieme, he would come back from a day at the Capitol exhausted, recalled his son Curt. Even though many considered him one of the best

CU ever had in dealing with politicians, Curt noted, "My dad often told me dealing with legislators was one of the worst parts of the job."

Buechner, a political science professor—former mayor of Boulder and state legislator—said, "Raut was my mentor." He was a "master at working with legislators, the governor and other political leaders—and alumni. In contrast to Curt, I never heard him say that he thought dealing with legislators was a difficult thing. Just the opposite. I thought he really enjoyed it. He liked politics."

Buechner thought that sometimes Rautenstraus could be vague about what he wanted him to accomplish with the legislature. One time he asked Raut to be more specific. He quickly responded, "Jonathan, I want you to get me another million dollars." Buechner smiled when he remembered, saying, "To me, that was pretty specific. I knew exactly what he wanted then."

Since Rautenstraus took over as CU's president, 1978 was the first year a significant part of the institution's request for increased funding from the state was not driven just by the cost of meeting physical plant needs and equipment upgrades. Prevailing cost-of-living expenses had seriously eroded salaries of key individuals.

Raut proposed correcting this. "I really am disturbed by the degree to which faculty salaries haven't kept pace with inflation over the last four years," stated Rautenstraus in a September 24, 1978 *Denver Post* article. "The urbane, soft spoken Rautenstraus," the article read, "stressed that his primary concern is that the average CU faculty pay has fallen some 15 percent below the median for state-supported members of the Association of American University—the prestigious group of 40 or more leading universities to which CU belongs."

He was concerned about getting and keeping the high level people he felt the University needed to maintain its quality and reputation. The chair of the CU-Boulder Faculty Assembly, Kaye Howe, echoed Rautenstraus' concern, saying, "In regard to pay, morale is very low and people are quite worried. We are losing ground with respect to the schools with which we compete. We're facing the time when we're going to begin losing people to other institutions." This was something Raut did not want his beloved school to experience. But the legislature and the governor would need to be convinced.

Just as he had done with the deans of men and women several years earlier, President Rautenstraus oversaw the merger of men's and women's athletic departments. The merger (which took place on July 1, 1978) was a move to comply with Title IX, a federal law requiring schools to offer equal opportunities in sports. "As part of the merger process, the two programs will coordinate their budgets to insure they reflect the real costs of competition and provide the maximum opportunities for both men and women to compete in intercollegiate athletics at the best level our resources will permit," stated Rautenstraus in a *Daily Camera* article (April 27, 1978).

Eddie Crowder, the men's athletic director since 1965, was named to head the combined department and Jane Wahl, the women's athletic director, was named assistant director. Neither Crowder nor Wahl reported receiving any criticism of the merger. However, this was certainly not the case concerning the current CU football coach's performance and his relationship with the media.

Robert (Bob) Six, head of Continental Airlines, was a staunch supporter—financially and otherwise—of CU activities, especially football. Six and his wife, actress Audrey Meadows, had been good friends with Raut and Willie for a number of years. They attended many CU events including football outings together. Six was unhappy with what was happening to the CU football program and had been complaining for nearly a year to Crowder about coach Bill Mallory. It was not just Mallory's win-loss record that had supporters like Bob Six infuriated. It was his attitude as well as his appalling relationship with the public and the media. Mallory asked Six for guidance on this.

In a December 20, 1977 letter, Six took Mallory to task for not coming around. He wrote, "First, let me say I am extremely disappointed in your reply after you asked for and spent one hour and 40 minutes with me on your personal and press relationship problems. To write me a letter reviewing that in one two-line paragraph certainly doesn't indicate that you have learned anything. Your letter shows absolutely no thought and depth whatsoever, and points out clearly that you have no sensitivity to people and no sensitivity to the problem."

He closed with, "Bill, there is not much more I can do at this point other than tell you that this year I will not participate in the CU program in any manner whatsoever. Please inform your staff there is no reason for them to call me or be in touch with me." Six sent a copy of the "personal and confidential" letter to Crowder and to Rautenstraus. Thus CU's president was brought into the loop of events that would fester throughout 1978 and would eventually result in Six sending letters directly to Raut. A Six letter to Roland on September 26, 1978 was copied to one of Bob's fellow CU booster colleagues, oilman Jack Vickers.

Six closed an October 20 letter to Rautenstraus—copied to Ira Rothgerber, a prominent Denver attorney and CU fund raiser—with these words: "I sincerely hope that the events that will be happening from tomorrow on will convince you and the Board of Regents that action should be taken on Bill Mallory in order to save what I believe will be a terrible financial situation." The next day, CU lost to Nebraska 52-14 at Folsom Stadium in Boulder. The team would go on to lose five of their last six games,

including their final game of the season to then-lowly
Iowa State 20-16.

The unpleasant state of affairs demanded action and
would finally lead to, not only Mallory's firing, but one of
the more extraordinary hirings of a coach in the annals of
college football. It would result in the University, its president, its athletic director and a leading CU football
booster being chastised in the national media.

10

RESIGNATION
(1978-1979)

B y the first of the year, the dispute between the University of Colorado and the New England Patriots over coach Chuck Fairbanks made headline news nationwide. Much of the news was unfavorable to Colorado and to its president. *The Washington Post* had reproached Rautenstraus on December 21, 1978, asking, "if he didn't regard a contract as a 'moral commitment' and if he had any qualms about the University seeking Fairbanks [while he was still under contract to the Patriots]." It posed the question, "Does a coach breaking a contract set a good example for students?" The CU president responded by saying he understood that Fairbanks had the right to leave New England and was working out the details.

Calling the incident "one of the most bizarre episodes in Colorado football history," Fred Casotti, in his book, *The Golden Buffaloes*, noted: "Eddie Crowder, seeking a big name to add quick glamour to the fading CU situation, came up with Chuck Fairbanks. Fairbanks had had fine success at Oklahoma before moving to New England and the National Football League (NFL), where he pumped life into the Patriots' program." Because the coach "was disenchanted with New England and the pros," Casotti said, "he came to quick terms with Eddie in mid-December." The Patriots had made it to the playoffs and wanted Fairbanks to stay to coach the team.

On January 15, 1979, "a federal judge banned the University of Colorado officials from trying to hire New England Patriots' coach Chuck Fairbanks and said they had been arrogant in their disregard for a legal contract," reported *The Washington Post*. "The preliminary injunction forbids CU Athletic Director Edwin Crowder, President Roland Rautenstraus, football booster Jack Vickers and the school's regents from entering into an employment agreement with Fairbanks." CU booster Bob Six was not named "because there was no evidence" that he had "directly contacted" the coach.

U.S. District Court Judge David Mazzone said "it was Crowder, Rautenstraus and Vickers, with the regents' blessing, who frequently contacted Fairbanks and urged him to go to Colorado." At the time of the injunction, the owner of the Patriots, William Sullivan, was hopeful he could persuade the coach to stay, "Time's a great healer. I'd like to think we could convince the guy to stay." That never happened.

After Sullivan and the Patriots "won some preliminary decisions," Casotti wrote, CU settled out of court. "Fairbanks gave up approximately $100,000 in deferred income to New England. And Colorado anted up a whopping $200,000." He added, "The Patriots were the first football team to collect ransom for a departing coach. And CU was $300,000 lighter in the bank account when legal costs were added to the payment."

The shame of it all was that Fairbanks only lasted three seasons and posted a dismal record of 7 wins against 26 loses. The most humiliating of the losses, which the consummate football fan Rautenstraus would have to endure while he was president, was a 13-9 defeat to lowly Drake, on September 22, 1979. CU was at "the school's gridiron rock bottom," in the words of Casotti—whose career at CU began in 1952 and who first served as its sports information director, then its associate athletic director.

In the first part of March 1979, a *Daily Camera* story by Sue Deans read, "People at the University of Colorado are mad as hell, and they're not going to take it anymore. That was the tenor of a massive campus meeting Wednesday, where at least 3,000 faculty, staff and students turned out to see what they could do about faculty and enrollment cuts proposed by the Colorado General Assembly." Action by the Joint Budget Committee (JBC) of the state legislature had recommended eliminating 10 percent of the CU-Boulder faculty.

"The audience hissed whenever the name of JBC Chairman William Hughes, a Colorado Springs senator, was mentioned," Dean reported. When Raut was introduced, the crowd cheered wildly. According to the *Daily Camera* article, "CU President Roland Rautenstraus, who announced his resignation Tuesday [March 7, 1979], was greeted with two standing ovations."

Raut addressed the crowd: "In the 15 years I've been involved with the JBC, I've never seen a set of recommendations potentially able to have such a profound and damaging effect on the University. I want you to keep in mind this is a marvelous place, and you are good. The simple fact that a few people say you are not that important does not make it so." He and the regents were deeply concerned "that proposed [state] cuts could cripple the state's higher education." Regent David Sunderland said, "The state can't have a first-class economy or living environment without full funding of the University. The prestige of CU comes from the quality and scope of its programs."

Upon hearing of Rautenstraus' resignation, Governor Richard (Dick) Lamm was quoted in a *Daily Camera* article by Carl Hilliard. The reporter stated that Lamm said CU's President Roland Rautenstraus "is the most talented, effective and knowledgeable president the school has had in years, and his resignation is a grave loss." The governor added that he hoped the president's resignation was "not because of spending limitations and enrollment caps proposed for the school by the legislature's JBC." But Lamm added he "believes it may be a factor."

Partly behind the JBC's recommendations to cap enrollments at the state's larger schools, reported Hilliard, was a determination that, for example, "lower division classes should be taken out of the University of Colorado's Denver unit and transferred to Metropolitan State, on the Auraria campus." To his credit, Lamm said he was not sure setting caps at the larger schools—CU, CSU, UNC—would force students seeking admission there to apply at the smaller colleges in the state. More often than not, those turned down by CU, CSU or UNC simply went to universities out of state.

Though the Colorado General Assembly only supplied about half of CU's operating budget of approximately $400,000 in 1979, its funding and support were crucial to the University's progress and success. In 1999, 20 years after Rautenstraus announced his retirement as president, the CU budget for all four campuses was more than $1 billion, with about $360,000 coming from the JBC. The state contribution for the Boulder campus itself would be less than 9 percent of its total operating budget, with the majority of its funding coming from research, gifts and tuition. And the cap of 20,000 students at the CU-Boulder campus would be a relic of the past before the century ended. None of this—a billion-dollar plus budget or elimination of the enrollment cap—was expected, though, in Raut's last year as president.

Rautenstraus' resignation "took most of the University community by surprise," commented the *Daily Camera*

(March 7, 1979). The Board of Regents Chair Fred Betz, Jr. reported, "As regents we are very concerned about this un-expected development. This has been initiated by Presi-dent Rautenstraus and not by the board or any member thereof." He was relieved that Rautenstraus had given the regents "a commitment to stay in charge until the search process [for his replacement] is complete," which would take CU through the current legislative season.

Most state legislators were pleased about this as well. "I'm glad to see that he is going to stay until a successor is selected. He is extremely effective with the legislature. He's well liked, and he knows his business," stated Sen. Les Fowler (R-Boulder). The University had been "in a virtual state of combat with the JBC over issues like the reduction of CU's faculty and enrollment." Someone with Raut's skills, demeanor and sense of history was needed to help re-solve the problems.

When asked why he chose to announce his resignation at the time when CU was in such a heated battle with the JBC, a "weary" Rautenstraus responded. He told Sue Deans, who wrote the March 7 *Camera* story, "I will con-tinue to serve as University president during the legisla-tive session. I really think all those matters will be resolved one way or another by the time this [his departure] takes place. Summer will come and most have to be resolved by then. During the summer and early fall, the new person can deal with the preparation of the following year's budget." His expectation that a new president would be named in that time span—and that he would never again have to get deeply involved in submitting another budget to the Colorado JBC—proved to be overly optimistic.

Regent Richard Bernick, who was completely surprised by the president's resignation, must have been looking into a crystal ball when he said, "I regret that we can't sup-ply a final few months of tranquillity [for Raut]." Regent

Jack Anderson said, "This man has done everything that was asked of him. I can understand his frustration and his desire to be relieved of this awesome responsibility." He added, "It has been a heck of a good five years [Raut's presidency]." And it was not over yet.

The March 11, 1979 *Denver Post* headline on Raut's resignation read, "Heading CU 'Constraining' (CU President Rautenstraus Found Office Too 'Constraining')." Art Branscombe, the *Post's* education editor, wrote, "Never has the University internally been in better shape, by most objective measures." As Rautenstraus saw it, "There is no doubt the national and international reputation of the University is higher than ever. There is very good acceptance by students. The general deportment of faculty and students is very, very high." Yet Branscombe also wrote, "Never since he [Raut] has been there, has it been under heavier attack by outsiders." And "as he [Raut] sees it: It is time for him to step aside."

The *Post* article continued, "A check of opinion among CU Regents, administrators, faculty and students reveals no one who shares his view that he should resign. And they are mystified by his decision. Rautenstraus seems to be regarded universally as an intelligent, humane person who has done a good job under trying circumstances. Perhaps the most telling words of praise for Rautenstraus came from Dan Caplis, president of the Boulder Student Union."

In Caplis' words: "He [Raut] has been available, accessible and straightforward. Whether we liked what he had to say or not, he always has been straightforward. He has been more accessible than some administrators at a lower level. Even students who weren't involved in student government could get in to see him, just students who wanted to talk to him about something. And the students who worked with him just loved him. I don't know how they'll replace him."

Point blank, Branscombe asked Rautenstraus why he resigned. Was it because of CU's ongoing fights with the JBC, the "interminable hassle" over the hiring of Fairbanks or something else? To the first question, Rautenstraus replied, "Well, obviously, I wasn't being as effective as I might have been, but that really wasn't the specific catalyst. It [resigning] had been on my mind at least six months. It was just a matter of determining when." About the football coach issue, he said grinning, it had no significance in his decision whatsoever. "I'm sorry that produced as much noise as it did. That certainly was not the institution's intent."

He then ticked off the three reasons he resigned: "First, I felt it would be better for the University to have a change. Second, I felt it was time I did something else. I just had my 55th birthday and I have found the presidency more and more constraining. I partially chafed at the feeling I was precluded from speaking out on a variety of public issues, not particularly connected with CU, by the possibility I might injure the University." Some of those issues, he iterated, were "higher education, natural resources, energy—about which I'm moderately knowledgeable and very much interested—and water.

"And third, as I've said before, I feel five years is enough. I've never done anything I prized as much or felt as privileged to do, but if there is any consciousness of over-staying my welcome, I think this is a good time to go."

About this, Branscombe wrote, "According to his bosses on the CU Board of Regents, Rautenstraus definitely hasn't overstayed his welcome." Bernick commented, "If there is any lingering suspicion that his resignation was solicited, I can assure it isn't true. If the board had its way, he would have stayed. I know the regents tried to talk him out of it [resigning]."

Reaching the age of 55 had a significant effect on Raut-enstraus, not only in his choosing to step down from the CU presidency, but with his personal lifestyle as well. It was reflected in the sale of his house. Turning 55, Ted Manning remembered, bothered Raut. It drove home the fact that he was human, time was ticking away and he was getting older. "A few month's before his birthday, he sold their house in Frasier Meadows and moved to a townhouse. Willie was a bit perturbed because if they had waited a few months—until he actually turned 55—their capital-gain taxes would have been nil. Raut didn't want to benefit from a tax savings if it meant he would have to say he was getting 'old'."

How Rautenstraus really felt about the Colorado General Assembly's heavy-handed attempts at micro-managing the state's institutions of higher learning came through in his last CU commencement address as president. Delivered at the summer graduation ceremonies in August 1979, his remarks had a sting to them:

"The more successful attacks [to destroy institutions of higher learning] are those which are subtle. They are the ones which may originate with elected and appointed officials who, under the cover of broad oversight and budgetary authority, promulgate rules, limitations, and regulations for the purpose of controlling the life of the institution in its most minute specifics. Individuals, for example, who themselves would find the notion of burning books to be offensive have no difficulty at all, either with their consciences or their constituencies, in cutting, earmarking and otherwise manipulating library budgets." (The entire address is reprinted in Appendix B.)

In a *Daily Camera* piece on November 15, 1979, he was quoted as saying, "Detractors may know the price of many things, but they know the value of very few."

Shortly thereafter in an accolade to Rautenstraus, State Sen. Jim Kadlecek wrote, "Best wishes to a good man." The senator confirmed that "running a huge institution like CU is not an easy task." Coupled with that, "he [Raut] also carried the responsibility of working with the members of the state legislature, who often think they know best how the school should be run. In that regard, I've found myself in the adversarial role that necessarily exists between the JBC of the legislature and the University over the dollars and budget needed to operate the institution. Usually, Raut, as the chief administrative officer, was the focal point of these discussions.

"Those debates have been particularly tense and difficult the last couple of years as higher education institutions are being forced to go through stringent external scrutiny as well as some soul-searching introspective. Through it all, Raut seems to have managed to maintain his outward calm and his genial demeanor. He is a sensitive and caring man and I'm certain he has withheld his feeling, when he felt he must, out of strong loyalty to the institution to which he is devoted. Raut is a good man; a strong positive contributor to our society. I wish him well."

Finally, on November the second, President Rautenstraus could see light at the end of the tunnel. The regents named his replacement: Arnold Weber, provost of Carnegie-Mellon University in Pittsburgh. Weber, who had a doctorate in economics from the Massachusetts Institute of Technology, was scheduled to take over in January 1980. Roland breathed a sigh of relief and prepared to take some time off before going back to teaching. Plus he had some other options to consider.

How Rautenstraus felt about engineers and the profession he reluctantly entered—but wholeheartedly embraced—came across loud and clear in the last major public speech he made as CU's top leader. The keynote speaker at the November 14, 1979 meeting of the Professional Engineers of Colorado, he said, "Young men and women choose the engineering profession largely as a result of the dazzling potential that it has to offer. It is a calling that views the world with a sense of wonder and delight, which challenges people to go beyond what is known, to do what has never been done before, to deny that things must always be as they have been.

"I think the single most valuable contribution the profession can make today is sharing its vision with the American people." How to do that, he stressed, "is to see to it that in public policy matters involving science and technology that the technical issues involved are clearly understood. The engineering profession must enter the political dialogue not only in an advocacy role but in an instructional role. Bringing these issues to the attention of decision makers should be considered as fundamental a responsibility of the professional engineer as voting.

"Second, engineers must recognize that engineering does not take place in a vacuum nor should it. The engineering profession itself must initiate the dialogue on the social, economic and political consequences of technological change. Finally, the engineering profession has a responsibility to share its vision of the future with the larger society. Engineers have tended to avoid doing this, perhaps because it requires them to become advocates for particular values ... and values are by their very nature somewhat intangible and irrational, something which makes professional engineers cringe. Nevertheless," he concluded, "it must be done."

On November 24, 1979, Roland's father Christian passed away. The 96-year-old theologian from the south of Germany, who had outlived his devoted wife by 18 years, had been living in a nursing home in Wheat Ridge. Raut and his brother and sister (Walter and Ruth), their families and a few friends attended the funeral. It was a quiet and modest event. Roland delivered the eulogy. It was loving and deeply heartfelt, but there were no public tears by Raut, remembered his son Curt.

11

THE MATRIARCH
(1980-1993)

T he beginning of the eighth decade of the century saw Colorado at the height of a modern day construction boom. There were so many construction cranes puncturing the sky in Denver and along the Front Range, many joked the "construction" crane should be the state's new state bird. The state's robust economy and growth, begun in the mid-1970s, was driven by the world's energy crisis. Projected energy development projects, including massive oil shale explorations on the Western Slope, seemed to indicate Colorado's present condition would continue well into the future. This forecast, unfortunately, proved to be utterly incorrect before the 1980s were half over.

Colorado's economy collapsed in the mid-eighties, just like those in other energy-based states like Texas, Oklahoma and Louisiana. For many years after the energy bust, major national lenders would not make "COLT" loans—loans for development and construction in Colorado, Oklahoma, Louisiana and Texas.

Upon Rautenstraus' departure as president, the University of Colorado and its 13th president Arnold Weber were finding that, even though—for the moment—the state's economy was booming, the availability of funds for its major universities was not. When it came to the state's institutions of higher learning, the Colorado Legislature, it seemed, continued to have a champagne appetite and a beer budget. The new CU administration soon discovered—and appreciated—how deftly and skillfully its last president had dealt with politicians and the public to get what money CU did get.

Ray Chamberlain, president of Colorado State University during the time Rautenstraus headed CU, said, "Colorado was a good school, but it was not truly recognized nationally prior to Raut's time. Now, CU—as well as CSU—is well up the list of the Top 100, class one research universities in the country. He [Raut] significantly contributed to that feat—getting Colorado to be a nationally and internationally recognized university. We shared some trying times together with state legislators. They just didn't always have enough money to go around: to both develop community and regional colleges, and fund the state's major universities. Raut was very effective in working with the legislature, getting what he could for Colorado."

Right after he stepped down—and for some time after—Rautenstraus was invited by several universities to consider becoming president of their institutions. Though he had stated early in 1979 he "would not go someplace else to be president of another university," he did consider other offers. Two he thought about seriously—even made visits to their campuses—were the university systems in California and Florida. He said, "At California, most of the chancellors were young. And it occurred to me that I had no political leverage there and I would serve at their largess. Here I knew people.

"And then when I went to Florida, the system looked so heterogeneous to me. I didn't like the attitude there and I was troubled with the sort of segregation that prevailed there then. And there were a bunch of other things." What those two experiences drove home to him, in the end, was this: "I knew then that I had no interest in administration anymore. I really just wanted to teach."

One of the main reasons he gave for this decision in a 1996 interview with Pam Penfold of the CU-Boulder Alumni Association was, "I was never sure what kind of administrator I was, but I was sure that I was a very good teacher. So I wanted to spend the rest of my life teaching engineering."

He admitted to a *Daily Camera* staff writer Janet Wiscombe on August 31, 1981—nearly two years after walking away from the presidency—that he was "a trifle fearful" at the prospect of returning to teaching. He had been in administration for 16 years. Changes—advances—had been going on in the classroom during that time, as they were in the civil engineering field. "The surprising thing," he told her, "was that the students were exactly as I remembered them. And not much in my subject field had changed. Terms, names—superficial things—had changed, not the basics. A lot of people who go from the classroom to administration believe in their own self-sacrifice. They believe they give themselves up on the altar at the expense of their subject field."

This, he felt, need not be the case. "There is real relevancy in much of what is done in administration. My administrative experience has had useful application in the conduct of the classroom." Always a master storyteller who could weave any tale with a message into an unforgettable lesson, Roland's moments at high leadership only added to his vast arsenal of anecdotes. Those experiences—his handling of such things as rioting students, short-sighted legislators, former chancellor Mary Berry, football owner Sullivan of the Patriots, and the construction of a major four-campus system—only added fodder to his legend with his students.

Even before Roland definitely settled on the direction the rest of his career would take—teaching at the University and doing some private consulting work—he made a commitment. Because much of his time would continue to be spent on the Boulder campus, he resolved not to publicly express "his views of the goings-on at the University." He expressed his stance this way: "I don't have much use for people who get out and persist in second-guessing what should go on when they are no longer in the arena." Nor, he added, did he have much respect for "those who have quit a job and sat back and complained about it."

That attitude, said Ray Chamberlain, was another one of the traits that displayed "what a true professional and gentlemen Raut was." Both Chamberlain and Rautenstraus were PEs (licensed professional engineers). They were heads of the two largest universities in the same state at the same time. It is probably the first and only time such a situation ever existed in any state in the nation.

The professors' desk in Rautenstraus' office on the fifth floor of the Engineering Center was small—not an inch bigger than that of any other faculty member's. It and the 10-foot by 12-foot room itself were a far cry from the baronial and massive trappings he had had as president. But he was totally content with the space, as he told anyone who cared to ask. He was there to teach students, not for fringe benefits. His salary as a full professor in civil engineering had been reduced to 80 percent of what he received as president. It was not a princely figure, but satisfactory.

During the Pam Penfold interview, Rautenstraus had recalled, "I was by far and away the highest paid member of the department when I went into administration. When I came back, I was just above the middle and when I retired (in 1993), two-thirds of the faculty were making more than me."

When asked why so many administrators cannot go back to teaching, Roland answered, "You have to be awfully sure of yourself as an academic because people don't accept you nicely when you return. You have somehow set yourself apart from them and they resent the fact that you no longer have goals that they can align themselves with. You have deserted them—crossed a line—and will never again be one of them. They don't look at you as an academic anymore; you are an administrator in their eyes."

Something else may have caused the division—real or perceived—in his case. He told Penfold, "When I went back to teaching, I told the department that I didn't want any of their meetings and their politics, so give me an extra course because I'm just here to teach." That Rautenstraus had no interest in faculty politics—or in second-guessing or meddling in the leadership of the department or the college—alienated some. It was appreciated, however, by most. When Roland returned to the college, the dean of engineering, Richard Seebass, noted that "Raut always called me 'Mr. Dean.' He was respectful, and a warm and kindly man. He never tried to abuse or take advantage of the power of his past position." And, he added, "he always received high ratings as an instructor from the students, even non-engineering students [taking introductory engineering courses]."

Hon-Yim Ko, chairman of the civil and architectural engineering department at the same time, echoed the dean's words by saying, "Raut was looked upon with awe, but he never forced his views on younger faculty. He would not barge his way into something, or onto someone. Nor did he intimidate anyone. He kept a low profile. But if you went to him for advice, he was always happy to take the time to help. He had a strong sense of historical precedent and could give insightful, wise counsel. On more than one occasion he advised, 'that won't get you anywhere,' and suggested a different tact, which would regularly prove to be the right one.

"Teaching—not administration—was his first love. His ratings from the students were always at the top. The nature of the courses he taught fit his style of teaching quite well: Introduction to Civil Engineering, Introduction to Building Construction, Technology and Society, Transportation Engineering, City Planning and Engineering Contracts (Law). In them, he could share his wide range of experiences, and discuss public policy and how to sell a project to the public. In the 1980s and 1990s, Raut was sometimes the only person teaching Introduction to Building Construction and Transportation Engineering—both required classes—so everyone who went to CU during that time would have had him for at least one class."

That Rautenstraus impacted many lives is a given. Just how significant that impact—or an encounter with Raut—was in the 1980s, after he went back to teaching full-time, is characterized by the following comments of Dan Norman (BSAE '88) and Kristy Schloss (BSCE '86). Norman had Rautenstraus as a professor in the second semester of his freshman year, the spring of 1984. "After a semester's futile struggle with the mysteries of computer science, I decided to concentrate my efforts on architectural engineering and as such had to take Introduction to Building Construction as a starter course.

"On the first day of class, in walked this serene, stately figure—Professor Rautenstraus. From the first moment he opened his mouth to speak, it was magic. Our engineering classroom was turned into a special experience. A couple of semesters later when I had him for Engineering Contracts it was as if we were taking a graduate law course at Harvard. And it wasn't intimidating at all. Raut had this grand way of making a course important while keeping it simple and relevant. Nothing seemed to give him more satisfaction than seeing the light bulb come on in someone's head."

Schloss added, "Raut encouraged us to be independent thinkers, to not only define the problems but also to determine how best to solve them. He always reminded us that there might be more than one solution to a problem. That was a different way of thinking than I had been used to: that there might be many different right answers. Raut was the most eloquent and well-spoken professor I'd ever had. I was an arts and science major before I transferred into engineering and there was no comparison: he was the finest. He excited us, inspired us and got us hooked into wanting to be the best we could be. I credit Raut with my passion for higher education and for confirming that a person can become anything he or she wants if they believe in themselves."

After graduating from CU, Norman and Schloss both stayed in Colorado. Kristy went to work for Schloss Engineered Equipment, Inc., a 100-year old Colorado-based environmental equipment design and manufacturing company (originally run by her grandfather). She eventually rose to the rank of president and CEO and was responsible for increasing the firm's international export sales by 900-percent in the past half-dozen years. In 1999, she and her company received the U.S. Small Business Administration's prestigious Small Business Exporter of the Year Award. Dan Norman, as was common for many of Rautentraus' pupils, went to work for a local consulting engineering firm to design major infrastructure projects in the state. In Norman's case, that included the three massive concourse structures at the $5 billion Denver International Airport.

Around 1982, close friends of Rautenstraus—George Maler and Ted Manning, in particular—noticed a major change in his demeanor. They noticed—as did others who previously had frequent contact with him like Regent Jack Anderson and Assistant Dean of Engineering Lanny Pinchuk—he was putting on a lot of weight. He had given up smoking in 1981 but that was not the sole culprit. It was also obvious he was dressing a lot more carelessly. Ted said, "He even gave up Cadillacs and started driving pick-up trucks."

But what really troubled Maler and Manning, and to a certain extent Anderson, was that Rautenstraus started distancing himself from them. They and their wives stopped doing things together with Roland and Willie. Rautenstraus, previously highly gregarious, became much more of a loner. They could not remember if this transformation was before or after one of the most major events in Raut's life occurred—but part of the reason for these noticeable changes was certainly linked to it.

On April 11, 1982, his dear sister Ruth died of cancer. She was 69. Over the years, Ruth had become the family matriarch. She acted, according to Raut's nephew Kent Rautenstraus, "as mother to Rolie because she was his teacher from an early age; he never wanted to do anything that would upset her." How Ruth felt about things was a driving force in everything her brother did, or would not do. She was strong, principled and ethical—like their parents—but Ruth was the biggest influence on Raut of the three. Roland's son Curt thought it was because his grandparents were "old fashioned—folks from the old country who didn't always communicate well with U.S.-born younger people." And that significantly factored into Raut's deep dependence on his sister for moral support and guidance.

A widow since 1975, right after Roland's presidency began, Ruth was often included at University events when Willie and Raut entertained. On occasion, she would accompany Willie to school functions Roland could not attend. One of those events, Willie remembered, was when CU played Army in football. "Ruth and I went to the game—flew on the same plane as the regents. I was the first woman that ever reviewed the troops," she joked. Ruth was along to back her up. (CU won the October 1, 1977 game, 31-0.)

At Ruth's funeral, Curt recalled, "My dad took Ruth's death pretty hard. Much more so than when my grandparents died." It was one of the few times Curt saw his dad "pretty much close to losing control." He was "on the verge of tears," but he did not cry—not in public.

Following the funeral, Roland called Ruth's son Larry Dumler and asked, "Would it be okay if I stayed at your mother's house for awhile?" While surprised by the request, he said, "Sure." Raut stayed in Ruth's house for about three weeks. After his mother's death, Larry recalled, "He [Raut] kind of isolated himself from everyone and very much withdrew." A doctor at the Boulder Medical Center, Larry said nearly everyone who knew Roland would ask when they came to the center, "How's Raut—is he all right? I haven't seen him for ages."

Willie and Roland formally separated in 1982. Their marriage had not been completely blissful for some time. Larry did not think it was unlikely that they had postponed their separation—while his mother was alive—because Roland was concerned about what her reaction to it would be. He verified that, even though his mother would probably not have condemned Willie and Raut for going their separate ways, she would not have been happy about it.

After the separation, Willie remained in the townhouse the couple had lived in since Rautenstraus stepped down as CU's president. He moved into a smaller townhouse in a different part of Boulder. Their condo in Vail, which Raut loved, became his, and he started spending as much time as

he could there. Much of it alone. Several old friends mentioned it was not unusual to run into him there—having
lunch or strolling along the streets of the ski town by himself. He was always gracious and constantly in a congenial
mood, happy to visit at length with whomever he met. But
he made no efforts to be any more sociable than that.

Raut and Willie never divorced nor lived together
again, but they remained friends for the rest of his life.
They would continue to have family gatherings together at
least once a year, usually over the holidays.

In the mid-to-late 1980s, Raut's health started failing
him. He developed diabetes and was having heart problems. He lost some of the weight he had gained after stepping down as president and bought exercise equipment.
But as Curt commented, "Dad talked a bigger game than he
practiced when it actually came to exercising." He had a
couple of minor heart attacks that, his son said, "required
him to take a lot of pills to treat. For some reason the
blockage in his veins couldn't be dealt with using angio-
plasty methods." He was not interested in having a bypass
operation. By then, he had completely stopped wearing a
tie—except for an occasional bolo tie—and had grown a
beard. It was gray. In the 1990s, he would wear his hair a
bit longer than was fashionable.

His weekly tennis matches became a thing of the past,
but he met regularly with a few of his old cronies—Jim
Corbridge and Lawson Crowe in particular—to play
snooker. Of the countless people interviewed about Rautenstraus, only two said he occasionally had a quick temper.
Just the opposite was true with virtually every one else; he
kept his cool under the most trying of circumstances.

The only situation mentioned when Roland lost his
temper involved playing snooker. Corbridge, who served in
several administrative positions including chancellor, is
presently a professor at CU's law school. He said, "Raut

had a real 'short fuse' when it came to snooker. If he made a poor shot, he would smack his cue stick against the table—often breaking or cracking the stick." David Grimm, who often observed the "friendly" pool matches, stated, "Raut must hold the all-time record for broken cue sticks at the CU Faculty Club."

Along with the snooker matches, the group of regulars—both players and observers—engaged in lively discussions on the hottest issues and pressing news of the day. They did not hold back their candid comments about the goings-on at the University and its reigning leaders. None of their remarks, however, were meant to leave the room, and they didn't.

As a "home-grown CU boy," Rautenstraus believed that when he retired from the head job—and remained on campus—he would be the institution's elder statesman, highly sought-after for his opinions. When that did not transpire, Corbridge felt Raut was somewhat disappointed and hurt. He never acted like it bothered him and he did not talk about it. "Even though he never tried to force his views on the new administration in any way, I think he was somewhat dismayed they never sought him out." He learned quickly how cruel it could be to be completely pushed to the side lines. It was as if retired presidents— even those that resigned and were not fired—dropped off a cliff, and were forgotten forever. Even as confident as Rautenstraus was, the situation must have caused him to reflect on his life's efforts.

Whatever was going on in his head as he distanced himself from in-laws and couples who were friends, two things remained constant: his love for being in front of students and the need for spending time with his son. Curt's wife Suzy had two children from a previous marriage. When she and Curt married, Raut sort of "adopted" her children as his "grandchildren" and became an indulging "grandfather" to them. He was with them as often as he could be, usually over the holidays and on special occasions. At events such as their grade school and high school graduations, Curt remembered, "Dad always showed up with presents and, though he was more subtle about it than with me, he visited with them about the value of getting a good education, how important it was for whatever they chose to do."

Curt recounted how excited his father became—even when he was in his late 60s—at getting ready for the first day of class each semester. "We would often have coffee [either in Boulder or in Louisville near Curt's office] after his 8 o'clock morning class, and dad would be really enthusiastic. He would have a twinkle in his eye when he told me, in great detail, what happened with his students. He always updated his notes, even for courses he had been teaching for years and years."

Their coffee-break meetings gave Raut the opportunity to regularly rib his son about how he was going to join his law firm, since he had an (honorary) law degree. This, Curt said, "he always did with that mischievous grin he got when he needled people."

Through all that was happening with him personally and otherwise, Rautenstraus continued to be involved with speaking engagements and public service. Governor Lamm appointed him to the Post-Secondary Educational Facilities Authority in 1983. One of its main functions was to help arrange financing for colleges—something Rautenstraus had mastered. In 1984, he was named to the Colorado State Bonding Authority, a position he held until his death. He was on the board of directors for several community groups, including radio station KCFR, Colorado Public Radio Network, the YMCA and the Rocky Mountain Writers Guild. In addition, he served on the United Way Campaign Leadership Team and the board of the Denver Center for the Performing Arts.

His consulting work in the 1980s and 1990s encompassed a wide array of activities as well. Roland continued to serve as a director for and work with Adelstein at Northwestern Engineering. He was an engineering consultant internationally as well, to groups like Nissan Motors in Japan, the Business Development Agency in Puerto Rico and Anwar Sadat's planning group in Egypt. He did much of his consulting work in the field of education.

Stein Sture recalled, "He [Raut] was passionate about his work with the North Central Accreditation Commission, from the early 1980s to 1994. He was president of the group for several years. They would do things like evaluate libraries around the country and work with local legislators to get funding, etc. He was also frequently called in by different universities to help settle a sticky situation. One of these involved being the mediator for a bitter dispute between the president of Georgia Tech and its Board of Visitors. It was a very difficult situation that required all of Rautenstraus' negotiation skills to help resolve. In the end, the president—who Raut thought was 'a crook'—was let go, at considerable expense to the university."

In 1993, 69-year-old Roland Rautenstraus retired. It was 50 years since he first stepped onto the Boulder campus and, of his half century at CU, nearly 48 years were spent as either a teacher or an administrator. Upon his retirement from the College of Engineering, the title of professor emeritus was added to that of president emeritus. Many would contend that the former (professor emeritus) rather than the latter emeritus meant the most to the man raised on the plains of Nebraska and Kansas. Retirement, however, for someone with his boundless energy—albeit poor health—would mean something considerably different than it did for most men his age. Raut would continue to teach engineering courses until his dying breath.

12

A LEGACY
(1993-1997)

After 1993, Rautenstraus reduced his teaching load but not his commitment to consulting work. Of particular interest to Raut in his later years was the transfer of technology. Many of his consulting assignments in this field were international in nature, requiring extensive travel. For someone who, in his younger days, would do almost anything to stay out of an airplane, air travel became a way of life for him in his twilight years.

How he became internationally well known in the area of technology transfer came about in a simple enough way. He confided to Pam Penfold (in 1996) that "I had written a couple of articles while I was president on how one transfers technology, particularly on how one transfers technology to non-technological environments. Because of that I became a fairly popular speaker for Third World ethnological development—how to enhance their economies."

In particular, he focused on countries in South and Central America. Raut worked extensively in Puerto Rico, where he helped construct several dozen manufacturing plants. He told Penfold he instructed the builders on "how they could make an industrial park, where to locate it and how to train people to work in it. In Puerto Rico, they have 50 plants and one in 10 Puerto Ricans works in those plants. But they are susceptible to other countries because of their reliance on those plants. They woke up one morning and two of their plants had moved, one to Haiti and the other to the Dominican Republic. That put 10,000 people out of work overnight.

"They asked me to come down and I did. I went to Haiti and the Dominican Republic and looked at their new plants. And they were just like those in Puerto Rico, but in Puerto Rico they were paying $6-per-hour and in Haiti they were paying 40-cents-per-hour. So I'm working with Puerto Rico now to see what they can do to sweeten the pot."

His consulting projects with Strategic Initiatives of Washington, DC and the National Center for Higher Education Management Systems (NCHEMS) of Boulder—up to his last days—not only delved into technology transfer but also policy formulation. He always produced an extensive written report with recommendations for the future for each assignment with these groups. Robert Lisensky, NCHEMS president, said Roland began consulting with his group in 1985 on a wide range of projects. "One that Raut really liked doing dealt with establishing an entirely new engineering college in New Jersey. It brought out the true engineer in him."

Not all of his clients were from the Americas. Rautenstraus told Penfold, "I'm a futures consultant in the western hemisphere for Nissan [in Japan]. I've helped Nissan locate plants in Mexico, Brazil and even in the U.S. Third World countries are where the manufacturing game will continue to expand. It's very ego-reinforcing when you go to some distant place and people listen to your recommendations—ideas that will have a major impact on their lives."

Part-time teaching and his consulting assignments were not the only things on Raut's plate in the 1990s. He was spending a lot of his time on two other favorite interests, the Colorado State Bonding Authority and Colorado Public Radio. The first group's activities included analyzing funding for post-secondary educational and cultural facilities, and certain public works projects like the Denver International Airport.

Colorado Public Radio president Max Wycisk said Rautenstraus was a mainstay on CPR's board for a dozen years. "He was very helpful in conceptualizing and formulating public radio in Colorado in 1983-4. Our board is made up of 20 people: lawyers, business people and community activists from around the state. Raut had this amazing ability to look at all the issues in a broad perspective and describe them with great clarity to everyone on the board, no matter what their backgrounds were. A lot of people can focus on their own concerns. He had this great intellectual capacity to see the whole picture and the communications skills to get others to do the same. He kept us focused on long-term development and looking ahead." Roland loved listening to classical music and Wycisk said, "Many of our board members were surprised to learn he was an engineer."

Just as in his school days, Raut had no difficulty meeting women in his later years. Stan Adelstein said that once Rautnestraus' marriage dissolved, Roland brought different lady friends with him to the Northwestern Board meetings. Adelstein noted that "they were always intelligent, mature and interesting women." Stan had a large pontoon boat on a lake in South Dakota. When the board meeting was held in Rapid City, the attendees gathered on it to relax and socialize after business was concluded. Stan recalled that Roland and his guest were always delightful conversationalists.

Raut attended Wheat Ridge High School's 50th reunion in 1992 with one of his high school girlfriends, Shirley Downs, who was widowed. After that, they went on picnics and to dinner a number of times. She said, "He usually had me home by 9 p.m." On one of their outings, they went to the Crown Hill cemetery where they visited first the grave of Shirley's mother, then those of Roland's parents and his sister Ruth. "Rolie told me he didn't ever want to be buried; he wanted to be cremated.

"Rolie was a very private person, even more so in his later years. He didn't go into too much detail about his personal life. I knew he and his wife were separated but that's about it. He was more unemotional than how I remembered him in high school. One time when we were out, I said something about his brother. Rolie told me he died. I asked him when and he said yesterday! (His brother Walter died on December 1, 1992.)* He said it with no real emotion. That struck me as odd. I thought there would have been some signs of grief or sadness, but there weren't." She added, "Rolie was extremely bright and perceptive and I admired the hell out of him, but things just didn't work out between us."

In the last several years of his life, Raut developed a close relationship with Sandy Hale. She accompanied Raut on many of his trips around the country and overseas, for business and pleasure and was his regular companion at social and academic events connected to the University. When Roland was in town, they had dinner together almost nightly, cooking at Sandy's house or frequenting lo-

---

*Raut attended Walter's funeral and burial at Crown Hill a few days later, accompanied by his estranged wife Willie. Kent Rautenstraus, who delivered his father Walter's eulogy, recalled, "Uncle Rolie was very gentle and tender. He really helped us cope with the moment. Rolie was like that, always a very caring and warm person." Kent gave the eulogy at Raut's funeral in 1997. It is reprinted, with his permission, in Appendix A.

cal Boulder restaurants. "Rolie was a good cook," she remembered. "He liked to prepare roast beef, pork tenderloins and macaroni and cheese."

Rautenstraus loved being outdoors. Hale's residence—a Victorian-style wood-framed house in downtown Boulder—has a small but pleasant yard. Raut liked to spend time in it, relaxing and helping with the yard work—trimming bushes and trees and even mowing the lawn. Hale said, "He didn't weed but he would come by to supervise to make sure we [Hale and her part-time gardener] worked hard and did things the right way."

The Remington Post condominium where Roland lived since the 1980s was a small place. He told Sandy that when he was president of the University he had a big house because it was necessary. Now, he said his small condo was all he needed. "That's all anybody needs. You don't need a big house," he said. One of the projects he gave his students was to prove how much space people need to live. In other parts of the world—everywhere but in the U.S.—people can get by comfortably with smaller homes, he would submit.

Raut always knew who he was. And he liked to hold court in social circles. In a group of strangers, he would eventually, if not early on, make his background—and that he had been CU's president—known to people. Hale said, "Often he would sit quietly for a while and, when it seemed appropriate, would start talking about some of his adventures. Everyone would gather around, fascinated. He was a wonderful speaker and was fond of telling stories. During the O.J. Simpson trial, with all the talk about the special Bruno Magli shoes, Rolie was tickled to tell friends that he owned a pair of Bruno Magli shoes too."

One thing Rautenstraus never talked about, however, was his pain—emotional or physical. "Rolie's diabetes made it difficult for him to walk, because he couldn't feel sensation in his feet," recalled Hale. He refused to use a cane in public, except sometimes walking in the mountains up around Vail. Sandy said, "He took medicine for his heart condition, of course, and he had slimmed down quite a bit in his later years. But Rolie never complained about his ailments. He was a very strong person."

In February 1996, the American Consulting Engineers Council (ACEC) honored Rautenstraus with its prestigious General Palmer Award for his many contributions to the progress of Colorado. Immediately prior to the awards banquet, Raut had been in the hospital for several days. When Curt drove his father home from the hospital the night before the ACEC function, he noted that he was still weak—and in frequent need of oxygen. Yet, Raut was determined to be ready for the event, and the next day he was. By the following evening, he recovered enough to attend the banquet. He, however, left his oxygen tank in the car because he didn't want any of the engineers in attendance to know he needed it. Most of them were quite surprised to learn that, just 24 hours prior, Raut had been flat on his back in a hospital.

One year later, right before CU's spring break in March 1997, the 73-year-old Rautenstraus called Stein Sture, chair of the civil engineering department, late one evening from Boulder Community Hospital. He told Stein he would not be able to teach his course in city planning the following morning. He said he had just been taken ill "with a very persistent ailment." Stein recalled, "He told me it was bronchitis or pneumonia, or something like that. He indicated he was just fine but felt weak. He would need to rest a couple of days in the hospital. He asked if I could inform his students and help find a substitute instructor. I told him I would, and for him not to worry and get some rest.

"Raut did indeed return to the college the following week. He showed up in the office looking rested and ready, as if nothing had happened. But he seemed to walk and talk a little slower. Later, I learned—not from Raut—that he had suffered a heart attack." Rautenstraus finished the spring semester, took time off during the summer and was back in the classroom for the fall term, to teach transportation engineering one last time.

Though Raut made several trips to Europe in his later years, he never tried to look up or visit with his relatives. It was almost as if he did not want to find out any more about where he came from than he already knew. He was comfortable with his memories as they were. On his second to last trip to Europe in 1965, though, he visited Germany to see the place where his father went to seminary school. "The rectors in two places knew my dad," he related to Penfold in 1966, "and they took me to see the apartment in Heidelberg where my dad lived when he was a student in 1908. I lectured in a room in which he had taken some classes."

The evening before Christmas in 1997, Roland did what he had done for years since he and his wife had separated. He went to Willie's house for Christmas Eve dinner. Present at the festive gathering were Curt, his wife Suzy and a few friends. Raut was in good spirits and talkative. Someone had asked him about his casino days in Las Vegas when he was a 17-year-old kid dealing cards. In the middle of his story, in mid-sentence, he just stopped talking and slumped back in his chair, unconscious. He was rushed to Boulder Community Hospital, but there was little hope. The old professor had had his final heart attack. Raut died peacefully on December 25, 1997—Christmas Day, one of his favorite holidays. The man from Gothenburg was gone. His legacy, though, was not.

At his request, Rautenstraus was cremated and his ashes scattered in a peaceful, wooded area at the edge of Boulder.

RAUT'S LEGACY

In reviewing Roland Rautenstraus' life, three basic observations surface. First, this was one extraordinary individual. His accomplishments are staggering. Second, the number of people he influenced is countless. And third, his impact on the University of Colorado and on the state—specifically its transportation and educational systems, and land-use policies—will be felt well into the 21st century. He was a visionary par excellence: "Never look at today for itself, always look at today as the beginning of something," he would say.

CU's 12th president came from modest beginnings, certainly. His family was not rich and famous nor were people around them. He grew up as a German immigrant's son during the Great Depression in small towns on the dusty prairies. And he was a teenager during the tumultuous years of WWII, just old enough to vote when it ended. Yet, his triumphs rose out of it all. Like other great men with similar lives, Roland had an unquenchable thirst from day one to meet challenges, and to become somebody. As CU Regent Jack Anderson said, "What drove Raut was not money, it was prestige."

Some of Roland's schoolmates in Russell, Kansas were exceptionally gifted and ambitious and, without a doubt, they and his older siblings influenced him. And he had fabulous mentors along his journey. Early on, he learned that the ability to speak well and perform in front of groups of people reaped big rewards. He never dismissed factors like hard work and being at the right place at the right time. But the main ingredient on Rautenstraus' list of things-to-do for success was to get as much education as he could and become the best he could at everything he chose.

His ability to talk eloquently—coupled with his theatrical skills—often got him noticed to begin with. His intelligence and insight, however, moved him to the top and kept him there. When he played football, he did not just show up. He gave it his all and, at times, even played with broken bones or other injuries, many times against much larger players. Though teaching (and practicing) engineering was not his original career choice, once he entered the field, he became magnificent at it. President Quigg Newton named him a full professor for his efforts when he was only 33, the youngest full professor at CU-Boulder. His peers on the engineering faculty elected him chair of the department two years later. All indicated his excellence at his profession.

The real confirmation of Raut's skills as a teacher, though, came from his students. First from 1946-64 then from 1980-97—with a 16-year hiatus in leadership in CU's administration—Rautenstraus taught thousands of students. He taught not just about engineering but about life and how important engineers were to society's progress. During his last years, he enjoyed teaching the grandchildren of men and women he first taught at CU. Of all the countless young people who had Rautenstraus as a professor, they have reacted virtually the same way: he was the greatest. He became, and remains, an icon to them.

Vince Kontny (BSCE '58) summarized it succinctly by saying, "Raut was someone every engineering professor should aspire to become. He made students proud of the profession and showed how engineering fit into the big picture of things. My son Michael (BSCE '97) felt the same way about Raut." Vince, who was the president of Fluor Corporation, one of the giants in the construction industry, added, "Raut is the only professor I really remember from my days at CU. It's because I used what he taught me in the real world. Typical engineering professors are too narrowly focused and technical. They don't motivate students to stay in engineering. He did."

Raut worked as hard, if not harder, at preparing for his classes in his later years as he did when he was a young professor. He frequently told people close to him, "I don't ever want them to take the chalk away from me." He did not want to be asked to leave because he had lost his touch as a teacher. Teaching was his fulfillment and it seemed to give him strength. He wanted to be in control of the decision of when to stop doing it.

When he stepped down as one of CU's youngest presidents, most observers were surprised. Many speculated on why he resigned at the height of his power. Adelstein, though, said he was not surprised, "Roland always said that the half-life of a CU president was only five years. Because of the University's system, its presidents are only truly effective for that amount of time." Planned or not, indications are Rautenstraus resigned the head post because he was weary of dealing with the politics of it all, tired of the constant battle with legislators over budgets and enrollment caps. He had a no-nonsense personality. It frustrated him to be unable to speak out on issues because it might cause problems for the institution he loved.

Why he stayed at CU instead of pursuing a similar leadership role somewhere else could easily be explained by saying he loved teaching so much, he just wanted to be a professor. That was much of it, but so was the fact that he was a pragmatist. He knew much of his effectiveness at the University came from being a "local boy" who knew Colorado. He was well respected by CU's alumni and had political clout in the state. Anyplace else, he would be the "new kid on the block" and would need to build a constituency from scratch. Plus he was not interested in getting into the cycle of looking for a new job every five years or so, as modern-day college-career presidents did.

In the final analysis, the answer became clear. During his early-to-middle life, he liked being comfortable and having

nice things—fine clothes and cars—but he was never moti-
vated to become wealthy merely to amass a fortune. (And in
his later years, he felt comfortable living simply.) He stayed
at the University because he was respected as its elder statesman and was free to do outside consulting work at his own
pace. When he coupled those factors with the fact that he
loved his full-time job—teaching young men and women—
the decision on how to spend the rest of his life was easy. Besides, teaching gave Roland the opportunity to perform on
center stage, something several people, including his wife
Willie, suggested he enjoyed immensely.

A private and complex man to the end, Rautenstraus,
like other notable men, had his human frailties—a few
kinks in the armor—but they never got in the way of his
mission. As the lines to "My Way" his favorite Frank Sinatra song go, his flaws and mistakes made were "too few to
mention." Through it all, Raut remained compassionate
and deeply concerned about people, especially those who
studied under him. He helped students—and his follow-
ers—reach for the stars. Anyone who came within his
radar screen benefited from knowing him. People could
look to Raut for inspiration, and to make them feel good.

The one solid thread running through—and linking together—Raut's successes as a teacher, administrator, engineer
and community leader was his golden oratory. That skill was
nicely described by his long-time friend Bud Davis—CU's
football coach in 1962 and now chancellor emeritus at
Louisiana State University: "Raut truly loved words. He
raised the joy of conversation to a high art whether he was
the speaker, or, better yet, the listener. He had the knack of
giving those in his presence the feeling they had his total,
undivided attention. His eye contact went to the bone. Thus,
whether one-on-one, in a crowded classroom, or in front of
a fulsome forum, he was ever the teacher and ever the
scholar—and his students and disciples loved him."

Raut's sincerity—along with his understated and informal management style—made him the champion for the common man (and woman). When he resigned the CU presidency, he took a cut in pay and walked away from the pomp and circumstance to pursue his passion: teaching. This act cemented his reputation for "class" and added to his legend as an American hero. And it placed him on the highest tier in CU's pantheon, a remarkable feat since his 16 years in administration were during very troubled times for the University of Colorado.

Other presidents' accomplishments have faded from the public mind but not his. In a story headlined "CU-President Relations Have Long Been Rocky" (in 1995), Carl Hilliard of the Associated Press reported, "If you took a look at the recent history of the University, there hasn't been a president who left under happy circumstances since Roland Rautenstraus. He had an engineer's aura of precise decision-making, plus calm and ability. Some folks think he should be hoisted on the shoulders of his admiring and considerable number of fans and carried bodily to the president's office. And thence to the desk and forced to serve again, whether he wants to or not."

Raut was a consummate doer, an engineer who showed up both to run things and to lead. He inspired with words and by setting an example. He did not just talk about doing something, he did it. If only three words could be used for his epitaph, they would be: teacher, leader, engineer, in that order.

In the end, CU's great communicator stayed true to himself and did things his way. He fully enjoyed the life he was meant to live. Roland Curt Rautenstraus, an elegant, caring man, unselfishly made the world a much better place because he lived.

■   ■   ■

Above: Christian Rautenstraus and Emma Stein engagement photo, Germany. c.1907. He was 24 and she was 19. Photo courtesy of Kent Rautenstraus

Left: Rev. Christian Rautenstraus, pastor of the Zion Lutheran Church, Gothenburg, NE. c.1920. Photo courtesy of Kent Rautenstraus

The Rautenstraus family (before Roland was born) in Gothenburg, NE. c.1920. Front (l. to r.), Herbert, Ruth, Emma, Walter. Christian is standing. Photo courtesy of Kent Rautenstraus

Roland as an child in
Gothenburg, NE. c.1924.
Photo courtesy of Curt Rautenstraus

The Rautenstrauses in Russell, KS. c. 1935-6. Front (l. to r.), Ruth,
Christian, Emma. Standing (l. to r.), Walter, Herbert, Roland. Herbert was
ill with cancer. Photo courtesy of Curt Rautenstraus

Four Rautenstrauses at home in Russell, KS. c.1938. (l. to r.) Walter, Emma, Christian, Roland. Photo courtesy of Kent Rautenstraus

The 1940 Wheat Ridge High School football team. Roland (No. 80, back row, right end) played guard and was named to the All-Central Suburban League All-Star team. Photo courtesy of Curt Rautenstraus

Typical engineering classroom at CU-Boulder. June 1945. Most students were Navy V-12 officer candidates. C.E. department head, Warren Raeder, is in the middle, front row. Photo courtesy of Stein Sture

Roland and Willie, during their college courting days. Spring 1943. Photo courtesy of Willie Rautenstraus

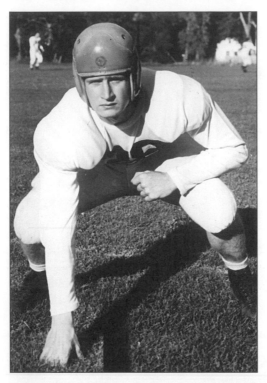

Left: Roland Rautenstraus lettered in football at the University of Colorado, 1943 and 1944. His uniform number was 38.
Photo courtesy of Willie Rautenstraus

Below: The Navy's Civil Engineer Corps Officers' School Midshipman Class No. Seven, September 8, 1945, Davisville, RI. Raut is in the top row, center.
Photo courtesy of Willie Rautenstraus

Above: Lieutenant Rautenstraus on Okinawa. 1946. Roland was an Assistant Civil Engineer in the Navy Seabees. Photo courtesy of Willie Rautenstraus

Right: Roland and Willie (Atler) Rautenstraus on their wedding. June 30, 1946. Wheat Ridge, CO. Photo courtesy of Curt Rautenstraus

The Christian Rautenstraus family. c.1949. Wheat Ridge, CO. Kneeling front (l. to r.), Willie, Curt, Raut. Standing (l. to r.), Larry, Ruth & Jay Dumler, Walter holding his daughter Diane, his wife Anne, Emma and Christian. Photo courtesy of Willie Rautenstraus

A 1955 surveying class, CU-Boulder campus. Raut (center at transit) and some of his students reconnoitering the fields where the new engineering center would one day go. It was one of the most surveyed plots of ground in Colorado. Photo courtesy of Curt Rautenstraus

The 1952 faculty of CU's civil engineering department. Seated (l. to r.), William Venuti, Leo Novak, Warren Raeder (head of the dept.), Wade Menoher. Standing (l. to r.), Roderick Downing, C.K. Wang, Ernie Leffle, Warren DeLapp, William Thoman, R. Rautenstraus, Roger Nelson, Gene Nordby, Jerry Passman, Kurt Gerstle. Photo courtesy of Stein Sture

Boulder City Planning Board. 1954-1958. Roland is third from the right. Photo courtesy of Curt Rautenstraus

Three heads of the Dept. of Civil Engineering in 1959. Front (l. to r.), Warren Raeder, Clarence Eckel, R. Rautenstraus. Raut had just been elected chair. Leaders of student engineering groups are standing behind the three. Photo courtesy of Curt Rautenstraus

Roland auctions off items at a backyard carnival to help his nephew Kent raise money for the Muscular Dystrophy Association. July 1972. Photo courtesy of Kent Rautenstraus

CU's Associate Dean of Faculties Rautenstraus with students at the Denver
Extension Center. 1967. Raut always had a special rapport with students.
Photo courtesy of Curt Rautenstraus

Curt, Willie and Roland in their new home at
Frasier Meadows, Boulder. Christmas 1970. His
nephew Kent, who took the photo, said Rolie and
Willie often had the whole Rautenstraus clan over
for the holidays, and their gatherings were always
grand events. Photo courtesy of Kent Rautenstraus

CU Pres. Rautenstraus and Gov. Dick Lamm leave the podium after delivering addresses at CU's commencement. Spring 1975. Former Gov. John Love (upper left) follows them down the ramp.
Photo courtesy of Curt Rautenstraus

Willie and Roland Rautenstraus. June 1974. He had just recently been named CU's interim president.
Photo courtesy of Curt Rautenstraus

President Rautenstraus at CU's Folsom Stadium. 1975. Ever the football enthusiast, Raut attended as many games as possible, supporting the Golden Buffaloes through thick and thin. Photo courtesy of Curt Rautenstraus

Folsom Stadium. 1975. (l. to r.), Rautenstraus, former CU Pres. Eugene Wilson, CU fund raiser Ira Rothgerber, CU football booster Bob Six.
Photo courtesy of Curt Rautenstraus

CU's 1975 Distinguished Engineering Alumnus Awardees. (l. to r.), Marion Dice, R. Rautenstraus, Alvin Swanson, Dean Max Peters (who presented the awards), Jack Hill. In the white suit is John Elliott's son, who accepted on his deceased father's behalf. On the far right is George Jenkins, chair of the college's engineering advisory group. Photo courtesy of Curt Rautenstraus

CU's 12th president with the Board of Regents. Summer 1975. Roland is in the back row, center. See Appendix B for names of the regents. Photo courtesy of Curt Rautenstraus

Above: Rautenstraus in the Honduras in 1976. Like a pied piper: everywhere Raut went, children found him fascinating and gathered around him. Photo courtesy of Willie Rautenstraus

Left: First Lady Betty Ford leaving the Rautenstraus home. Fall 1976. She stayed in Boulder as the guest of Roland and Willie. Photo courtesy of Willie Rautenstraus

Raut (right) receives an honorary degree—Doctor of Laws, honoris causa
—from the University of New Mexico (UNM) in 1976. William (Bud)
Davis, president of UNM (center) makes the presentation. Photo courtesy
of Curt Rautenstraus

Africa, 1977. On behalf of the U.S. State Department, Raut and presidents from several American universities visited African nations. Raut's
luggage was lost some place between New York and Egypt and he spent
the entire trip wearing one suit, which he promptly discarded upon
returning to the U.S. Photo courtesy of Curt Rautenstraus

Regent Fred Betz, Jr. (right) reads the citation and presents the prestigious University Medal to Rautenstraus (center). May 1979. Photo courtesy of Curt Rautenstraus

CU past presidents, Rautenstraus (left) and Quigg Newton (center) congratulate Stan Cristal at the dedication ceremonies of the Cristal Chemistry and Bio-Chemistry Building. September 1994. Photo courtesy of CU-Boulder Alumni Association

The College of Engineering's Centennial Medal is presented to
Rautenstraus. 1994. Congratulating Raut (left) is Lanny Pinchuk, assistant
dean. Dean Richard Seebass (center) looks on. Photo courtesy of Sandy Hale

Roland relaxing in Vail, CO. c.1995. For many years he had a second
home in the mountain resort. Photo courtesy of Sandy Hale

Above: President Emeritus Rautenstraus delivering the August 1992 CU commencement address. Photo courtesy of CU-Boulder Alumni Association

Right: The General Palmer Award was presented to Raut (left) in February 1996 for his lifetime achievements. CU's dean of engineering, Ross Corotis (right), shares the moment with him. Raut had just been released from the hospital the night before the presentation. Photo courtesy of American Consulting Engineers Council of Colorado

APPENDIX

APPENDIX A

RAUT REMEMBERED: ADDITIONAL THOUGHTS

STAN ADELSTEIN
(BSCE '53, president of Northwestern Engineering Company and chairman of Hill Materials Company, Rapid City, SD)

"Roland had a magic way about him. He was incredibly articulate, and is the model for the profession. He enjoyed public service and his participation on public boards drove home the point that engineers can make society much better. Because of their education and logic, engineers can improve a system that would otherwise be a system illogically based."

ED BANKS
(Raut's assistant, 1968-80)

"Raut's leadership style was to never act like he was the boss—he low-keyed that fact, even when he was president. He was an excellent delegator. Because of his style, everyone did their very best and always made that extra effort. They not only worked harder for him than anyone else I've ever been around, but they enjoyed what they were doing more. Everyone, even those on maintenance crews, would say, 'I worked *with* Raut,' and never, 'I worked *for* Raut.' Raut really loved the University and its students. He very much enjoyed being president, but he didn't want to do it for his whole life. He was the happiest man in the world when he could teach full-time."

PAUL BARTLETT
(Dean emeritus, College of Engineering, UCD)

"He was always supportive of people—seldom missing the opportunity to congratulate them on a promotion, award, etc. Raut usually asked that papers be mailed to him, rather than put them in his pocket, so he wouldn't misplace them. He often asked to borrow a pen or pencil as he frequently left his at his office. Words to put on his epitaph would be: Engineer, Professor, Administrator, Humanitarian, Patriot, Author, Philosopher. Knowing him was a wonderful experience."

RICHARD BERNICK
(Denver attorney and three-time regent, including during the Rautenstraus' presidency, 1974-80)

"I think that the major distinguishing characteristic of Raut from the other presidents who preceded him and followed him was his genuine love for the students, his recognition that the University existed for them, and his tremendous loyalty to, and love for, the University. Of course, all presidents tell of their love for students and for the University, but none of them that I know of have demonstrated that as fully as Raut."

JOHN BUECHNER
(President of the University of Colorado)

"A decisive person with a powerful voice who stood tall in any situation would be a good way to describe Raut. He had a very good vocabulary. He could take almost any mundane subject and, through his use of words, make it sound a lot better than it was. Yet, even though he was extremely articulate, he did not go into battle unprepared—he was not a hip shooter. He'll be remembered as the calm, even-tempered engineer who developed the CU system as we know it today. From a leadership point of view, Raut's style of management was one that allowed those under him a great deal of latitude. He'd say, 'Here are your tasks and I'm going to allow you to develop them. I'm going to support you, but you're going to be held accountable for your actions.' As a person, he had an amazing way of making those around him feel at ease and comfortable no matter how tense the situation might be."

ED CARPENTER
(Colorado state legislator, 1985-88)

"Raut was still remembered and greatly admired by the legislature several years after he stepped down as president of CU. He was at many of the receptions the University had for we legislators and his ideas and visions intrigued our imaginations. Raut was always after me to serve on the JBC so I could better influence how the state funded its institutions of higher education."

RAY CHAMBERLAIN
(President of Colorado State University, 1969-80)

"During the period that Raut and I served as president of CU and CSU, respectively, I felt that he not only served as a strong advocate for CU, but he also was a leading public figure on behalf of all higher education in Colorado. Further, Raut was an outstanding teacher himself and always asserted the importance of teaching being done by all who were members of the faculty."

JIM CORBRIDGE
(Former chancellor of UCB)

"Raut was a very private but warm person, a good man who impacted a lot of lives, mine included. Raut wasn't stuck in the dark ages—he was extremely adaptable and flexible, willing to embrace new methods. Plus, he had a keen political sense and knew the history of the place better than anyone. Under his leadership CU made great strides forward, and he was always proud of that fact. Raut was a colorful, dashing figure who took an intense interest in everything he did, even playing snooker."

LINDSAY COROTIS
(BSCE '99)

"Professor Rautenstraus never used the chalk board nor overhead slides, he just lectured. [Lindsay took the last course Raut ever taught the fall of 1997, Transportation Engineering.] He taught us not only a lot about transportation in the U.S., but also about how it's done in other countries. He got us thinking about the pros and cons of the European train systems, mass transit and international air travel. He always had time for students, and we respected and loved him. Students can tell when a teacher wants to be in class, Prof. Rautenstruas was truly someone who wanted to be there. It was because he really liked teaching. You could tell every day he walked in that he was having fun."

PAUL DANISH
(Special secretary and speech writer for Rautenstraus, 1977-80)

"To him the journey was more important than the prize. He had that talent to bring out the best in you. He asked the right questions. The University was so much a part of him. What he liked least about the job of being president was the intrusions into one's privacy. He was a very, very private person."

DEL DAVIS
(BSCE '59, former CEO, Ball Corporation)

"He was undoubtedly the best instructor at the University, the best, by far that I've ever encountered—a great educator with a gentle soul. He was a man who could efficiently keep many 'balls' in the air simultaneously, i.e. be a teacher, chair a department, oversee student activities, and be a consultant and leader."

WILLIAM (BUD) DAVIS
(Chancellor Emeritus Louisiana State University, former president of the University of New Mexico and author of *Glory Colorado!*)

"When the history of that great university—Rautenstraus' great university, the University of Colorado—is written, the time of Raut's administration will stand forth as the years when the institution made the transition from the Boulder campus with outlying branches to a University of Colorado system with a central administration and president overseeing multiple, full-blown, degree-granting campuses administered by chancellors. It will also mark a time of emancipation of the student from the shackles of *en loco parentis* to an increased awareness of, and sensitivity to, the issues of diversity, equity, justice and humanity. If students were the marchers, Raut was their pied piper."

EDITH DELL'APA
(President of University of Colorado's Women's Club, 1983-4)

"Roland had the ability to get along with everyone, from top executives to students. His rapport with the students when he was president—and executive vice president—was outstanding. He talked their language which kept them calmed down and their campus demonstrations peaceful. Roland was interested in so many things—music, drama, opera, sports, education, politics and what was going on in the community. He was truly a renaissance man."

PETER DIETZE
(Boulder attorney and CU regent from 1979 to 1996)

"It was his loyalty to the University that stood out. Raut was a warm, kindly and cordial man whose laid-back style of leadership worked well during the troubled times CU went through in the 1970s. He did not leave the presidency because the ship was in trouble. It was solely his choice to resign."

DAVID FOWLER
(Joe J. King Chair at the University of Texas-Austin, Ph.D. in CE from UCB, 1965)

"One of the reasons I went to graduate school at the University of Colorado was because of Rautenstraus. He convinced me that CU had a leading-edge engineering college, and that it was only going to get better. Raut was extremely articulate and made an excellent impression on people. He had one of the most pleasant demeanors of anybody I've ever been around. Once you met him, you always felt good just to be in his presence. I don't ever remember hearing anybody say a bad word about him."

NATHAN GALLEGOS
(BSCE '99)

"He was a really good professor, and a very personable guy who was pretty wise. I never remember him writing on the board once. He would just get up and talk, at a pace where we could get our notes down. His exams were based entirely on his lectures. He'd relate real-world stuff like the 'right of eminent domain' and how it was used in the construction of U.S. 36 and certain CU projects. Professor Rautenstraus really enjoyed teaching—and telling stories about the projects he worked on. He had a story for every lesson, some of them were quite comical. He was pretty laid back and casual, and straightforward. He lectured more as a friend than a professor."

DAVID GRIMM
(Rautenstraus' special assistant, 1974-80)

"Raut was one of those incredible people who had the ability to step outside of himself and bring forth the best in others. He was not a worrier. Raut saw being president of CU, not so much as the pinnacle of his career, but as one event in his journey of life. He loved being an integral part of the University, though, and he 'read'—and related to—its culture better than anyone, before or after him."

ED HAASE
(BSCE '44, former CU classmate of Rautenstraus and chief engineer for the Colorado Department of Transportation)

"Raut was an excellent student, a fine academician and great pragmatic. He quieted a restless campus as president. I always hoped he would be appointed Executive Director of the Colorado Department of Transportation when he stepped down from the CU presidency. He would have been a great one! His support for a sound transportation infrastructure system in Colorado never wavered."

SANDY HALE

"Rollie prided himself on his choice of words. It became a joke between us when I occasionally corrected him and he always reminded me that for most of his life he was widely regarded as the ultimate wordsmith. Consequently, when he died and I remembered him with a special brick in the Chautauqua Park Memorial Path. I had it inscribed, Roland C. Rautenstraus Beloved Wordsmith. When Rollie spoke of his childhood and family, which he often did, he always spoke fondly and proudly of his parents." (According to Sandy, Raut's remembrances of his childhood were that his parents had many friends. She said he told about "many adults [artists, schoolteachers and the like] who sometimes lived in their home.")

JOANNE JOSELYN
(Space Scientist, National Oceanic and Atmospheric Administration. Boulder, CO)
(*In 1961, JoAnne was in a special class of 30 advanced honor students at CU, enrolled in Rautenstraus' course, "Technology and Society."*)

"I had recently learned to knit and thought it was cool to knit while in class. One day I did that in Raut's course. He saw me, stopped lecturing, and came over. He had me put my knitting away and said, 'Young lady, don't you ever do that again.' I was so nervous my knees were knocking. And I never did that again. Raut was such a wonderful teacher and he really got us all so enthused about how technology and engineering were so critical to society and civilization. One of the best papers I've ever written was based on what I learned in his class."

HOWARD KIRKPATRICK
(BSCE '50)

"I had Professor Rautenstraus for several classes and never heard anyone calling him 'Raut' [back in 1950]. The first class I had him for was Surveying. He showed us how to throw the range pole like a javelin—javelin style. After about an hour, he told us that if he saw anyone doing that, he would fail the course on the spot. Rautenstraus' favorite expression was: much to my chagrin ..."

HON-YIM KO
(Chair, UCB Department of Civil, Architectural and Environmental Engineering, 1983-1990, 1998-present)

"In the large sense, Raut remained very steadfast in keeping with his goals of education. He never got sidetracked by those clamoring for more and more research. To him, teaching students should remain the main goal of professors. I don't think he would like the current CU policy of professors only teaching three classes so they can have more time for research. He always felt his contribution to the department was to teach—to be the best teacher he could be. He was an extremely tolerant person, very philosophical. When you were in a room with him, he made you feel totally comfortable."

VINCE KONTNY
(BSCE '58, former president of Fluor Corp., Irvine, CA)

"He had wonderful people skills—he made everyone in his presence feel special. When he talked about something he made it interesting and intriguing, you wanted to listen close and learn more. The last time I saw him [in 1992]—it had been more than 35 years since I took a class from him—he called me by name. He said he remembered everyone he taught but I wondered.

Then, he told me a few things I did in class that only he would know and I was convinced. He had a fantastic memory."

RICHARD D. LAMM
(Former governor of Colorado)

"Roland was always there when the State of Colorado needed him. He served us honestly and well, and made great contributions to my administration and the State of Colorado."

TED LASZLO
(BSCE '99)

"Learning from Professor Rautenstraus was very special and informative because he had so much experience with transportation, from its early days on. [Ted took Transportation Engineering from Raut in 1997.] He was quick to offer stories that helped people learn, plus they were extremely interesting. I think it would be almost impossible to find anyone who didn't like his class. Prof. Rautenstraus told us that at his age [73] he was pleased to be able to mingle with the younger generation, and hopefully influence what would come out of our collective minds. He wanted to stimulate our thoughts and our vision for transportation of the future."

ROBERT LISENSKY
(Past president of NCHEMS, Boulder, CO)

"My memories of Raut cover the years he served as an NCHEMS consultant [1982-97]. His wisdom was a unique mixture of the practical and the professional. But what I remember most are the personal conversations we had at dinner after our work day was over. He liked to recount his days as a boy—how, because his father was a Lutheran minister born in Germany, their home was a haven for distinguished visitors, especially from Germany. Raut listened and participated in their discussions. These early life experiences stayed with him. He was always open and respectful toward people whose thought and culture differed from the 'norm.'"

JOHN A. LOVE
(Former governor of Colorado)

"During my tenure as governor I had many, many occasions to deal with Roland about problems and challenges faced by the University. On all those occasions I found him not only well aware of the problem but able to find a solution. He did an excellent job as president and served the University with distinction."

RICHARD MAIRES
(BSCE '53)

"Professor Rautenstraus was the type of teacher you could kid with—and he with you. But you always knew he was boss. What he taught, you learned. Raut taught surveying and in our class [in 1950] there were several of us who were skiers. We kept kidding him we would cut Fridays (to go skiing) in the hope we would get his tacit approval. But he said, 'If any of you miss Fridays, I'll flunk you.' We never missed a class."

TED MANNING
(CU Vice President and Dean of Faculties, 1964-71, President of University of Bridgeport in Connecticut, 1971-75)

"Raut thought it a great opportunity to be president, then he discovered it was not all that much fun, and not that rewarding. He was a quiet, self-contained person—honest, perceptive, dedicated and with high integrity. He was a private man who did not talk of personal things and, often, you had trouble finding out what he was thinking. Raut liked history, especially local history. He belonged to the Colorado Historical Society for years and, up in his home in Vail, his bookshelves contained a full collection of Historical Society Journals."

DWAYNE NUZUM
(Director of CCHE, 1994-99, dean of CU's school of architecture, 1970-80)

"I took 'Strength of Materials' from Raut while I was studying architecture at CU. Through the years, Raut was my mentor and good friend. He was a one-of-a-kind person, someone who could laugh at himself—who didn't have to be serious all the time. When we played together as doubles partners in tennis he would say, 'Nuzie—he had a nickname for everyone—I'm going to guard the double's alley so they don't fool us with a shot down the line. You stay alert and take care of the rest of the court [the majority of the tennis court].' Raut was a super president for Colorado. It was because of his strong leadership that the University was able to heal [from the disruptions of the 1970s]."

LAURIE PADDOCK
(Editor emeritus, *Daily Camera*, Boulder, CO)
*(At Rautentraus' retirement party in 1980, Paddock presented a
humorous slide show of Raut's life. The following is from that
presentation.)*

> Things that Roland will be remembered for: "His appearance—his
> demeanor—his golden tones—his unusual pronunciation of
> AGAIN —-his repeated use of the word SCENARIO and the term
> THE ENTERPRISE."

LANNY PINCHUK
(Assistant dean of engineering, UCB, 1987-91)

> "Raut captivated people. He was a fascinating individual and a
> spellbinding storyteller. He never lost his down-to-earth attitude
> nor was he ever anything other than who he was. There wasn't
> an ounce of snobbishness about him. Even when he was presi-
> dent, Raut never put on airs, although he may have sounded like
> it because of the sophisticated way he talked. He was a really
> good human-being whose persona was never affected by his po-
> sition. Raut didn't treat anyone as being beneath him. It was one
> of the reasons students fell in love with him. Raut, in the final
> analysis, was basically an introspective person, someone who
> had deep feelings and emotions for other people."

KENT RAUTENSTRAUS
(Raut's youngest nephew)

> "He was just the magical uncle. Just his style, his playfulness and
> the way he always kidded. He had terms of endearment for each
> of us and teased us. He was such a trend setter with his fashion
> and coats—and even later when he let his hair grow long and he
> had that scruffy appearance. He loved to eat good food. His in-
> tellectual curiosity: he had a brilliant mind. He was always pon-
> tificating to the family about natural resources and over popu-
> lation—and things like light rail. He was always saying 'we've
> got to watch out for these things.' Rolie and Willie often had the
> whole family over for holidays and they spared no expense in
> creating memorable parties. On several Fourth of Julys he in-
> sisted we all go to see the CU fireworks show and Rolie was like
> a kid, enthusiastic about each new shower of fireworks."

WILLIE RAUTENSTRAUS
(Roland's wife)

"He liked politics. At one time, he talked about running for governor. He would have liked being governor since he loved Colorado so much. But nothing ever came of it, mainly because he started having health problems, first with his heart, then later on he got diabetes."

KRISTY ANNE SCHLOSS
(BSCE '86, president and CEO of Schloss Engineered Equipment, Inc., Denver, CO)

"Raut was revered and respected by students—treasured for his knowledge, and his eloquence. When he taught us about the U.S. Interstate Highway System, he didn't just go over its technical details, he told us about the thought behind it, and how it came about. All his wonderful stories kept us riveted, and we were enthralled by his every word. Every one he used was calculated for maximum effect. Raut set an example for what engineers can accomplish. He was certainly a role model of someone who gave back to his community and society, and he instilled in us the concept of the engineer as a community leader. Because it's really engineers who are key to society's quality of life, he said engineers have larger responsibilities [and talents] than those of just serving as designers and servants. Their greater calling is as industry and community leaders."

JOE SICCARDI
(BSCE '49, former chief bridge engineer for CDOT)

"He never forgot you, even after he became president. I took surveying from him way back in 1947. For a number of years in the 1970s, I taught at UCD and one evening, Raut saw me through an open door and came into my classroom to say hello. He told the class I was his former student and visited with them. My students knew of him and were impressed. He was a giant of a person—and the students' professor."

JOSEPH R. SMILEY
(The 9th president of the University of Colorado, 1963-69)
(Smiley brought Rautenstraus into CU's administration in 1964 by selecting him as associate dean of faculties. The following is his endorsement of Roland for CU's prestigious Norlin Medal.)

"I found Raut to be invariably dependable, cooperative and honest, and his assistance and counsel were invaluable to me as we worked through a variety of situations and problems. In short, I have the highest regard and respect for his capabilities and performance. His long and distinguished service to the University in academic and administrative capacities, his professional status and contributions to engineering, his wide and favorable acquaintances among the University's alumni serve to make him eminently qualified for the Norlin."

FREDERICK THIEME
(The 11th president of the University, 1969-74)
(The following comments were recorded by Ronald James in Our Own Generation. *Thieme's remarks were made to clarify why he selected Rautenstraus to be his executive vice president.)*

"Raut was old CU. I never doubted his affection for this institution, and I found his background so deeply embedded in it that I used him quite heavily to represent those kinds of traditional interests of the University. Raut also had a knowledge of alumni and people who know the University. I had to have somebody around me that I could ask what about so-and-so. Raut represented that resource."

JOHN D. VANDERHOOF
(Former governor of Colorado)

"My personal contacts with Roland over the years have been many and pleasant. It was for this reason that I appointed him chairman of the transportation committee of Colorado's Energy Task Force. His services to the cause of higher education, both as a teacher and as an administrator, are undeniable."

MAX WYCISK
(President of Colorado Public Radio, CU Ph.D. English '72)

"What I consistently admired about Raut was the depth of his thinking: his ability to describe the essence of an issue, and then very calmly to propose a solution. He was almost always right. He was a truly amazing man."

EULOGIES AND MEMORIALS

EULOGY BY KENT RAUTENSTRAUS
(December 29, 1997)

"The Rautenstraus Family Remembers
Its Most Colorful Relative,
Roland C. Rautenstraus"

The noted theologian Peter Marshall once said, "The measure of life, after all, is not its duration, but its donation."

I am honored today to share on behalf of the entire Rautenstraus family some thoughts and remembrances about my Uncle Roland. Before I relate some family memories, I'd like to convey messages from three individuals who knew Roland in a personal or professional capacity.

Saturday, I spoke with Senator Robert Dole's younger sister, Norma Jean, who still resides in Russell, KS. She remembered Rolly as quite an energetic kid! She put me in touch with the Senator's personal aide, Marcie Adler, who resides in Washington, DC. She contacted Senator Dole, who was on vacation for the holidays.

He was saddened to hear of Roland's death, and sent this message through his aide, "Senator Dole sends his deepest sympathy to Willie, Curt, and the family. The Senator remembers the good times when he and Roland were young boys and young men growing up in Russell, KS, and he has warm memories of Roland and fellow classmates Henry Bender, Adolph Reisig and Phil Ruppenthal. He will be thinking of you all on Monday morning." You may have noticed the bouquet of sunflowers. They are the Kansas state flower, and were sent with condolences from Senator Robert and Elizabeth Dole.

Dr. Richard Bond, former President of the University of Northern Colorado, asked me to convey his sympathy to the family. Recalling a difficult period in the late 1970's, Bond reflected last night, "Raut provided an incredible amount of leadership in bringing the presidents of the universities together. It was a time of tough funding and we had to convince the legislature that they could let go of some of the strings because the leadership of the universities was trustworthy, and Raut played a large role in that."

He made some other comments, and then said something that I thought really captured the essence of Uncle Rolly. "I particularly enjoyed Raut's affability. It was the right amount of seriousness and frivolity, and the right amount of profoundness - and sometimes plain baloney!" He concluded with "He contributed mightily to the growth of higher education in this state, and he's high in my regards."

Governor Roy Romer also telephoned this message to the family. "Roland Rautenstraus was a creative educator in Colorado. He helped me many times puzzle through tough questions on higher education. Also, I remember his tremendous sense of humor. He was a true friend of mine, and a friend of Colorado's."

As a family, we all have wonderful memories of Roland. Here are some of his characteristics and qualities that most stand out (in no particular order of importance):

- **A gracious host.** He and Willie were *the* consummate hosts who made family gatherings very special and memorable. Every detail was perfect and money was no object. My mom, once, gave this description of a holiday gathering, "You'll remember Willie and Rolly for their unique candelabra with tiers of red and green candles, the chocolate-covered orange sticks made at Manuels in Boulder, and the superb food served so elegantly. Afterwards, Rolly would push in the cart loaded with after-dinner drinks and another log would be thrown on the fire before opening gifts."

- **A tease.** Rolly was always kidding us and making up nicknames. Sue Dumler was forever "Suzy Bell" and I was "Kenter" to name just two. He referred to Suzy Rautenstraus as "his *favorite* daughter-in-law". To my wife Kathleen, he teased her by predicting that we would grow tired of our house and move on to a bigger and better place within seven years. (We're coming up on seven years, and don't have any intention of moving!) And when he purchased the gigantic red pick-up truck that he loved so dearly, he couldn't help but gloat, proclaiming gleefully that it was "the largest truck in the family!"

- **A trend setter.** We well remember Rolly's personal sense of fashion. The man was a snappy dresser! His plaid coats are forever etched in our memory! More recently, he let his hair grow long, and when he grew a beard, some said he took on a scruffy appearance. We preferred to call it his 'professorial' look!

- **A lover of good food.** Whether it was selecting the finest and thickest cuts of meat to barbecue, or dining at The Red Lion, one of his favorite restaurants, food was a special joy that Uncle Rolly shared with his family.

- **A man of intellectual curiosity.** Rolly was a deep thinker. His nephew Larry called him a bit of an "intellectual doomsayer" for he had genuine concern about the depletion of our natural resources, the energy crunch, problems associated with over-population, and current challenges with higher education and light rail.

- **A charmer who loved holding court.** On the before-mentioned topics and any number of other trivial and banal subjects, Rolly loved to 'hold court'! At our family gatherings, a group would always be gathered around Uncle Rolly to get his take on a particular current event or issue. He had a brilliant mind and he was an engaging and knowledgeable speaker. He was also a good bluffer. Willie once half-jokingly said that Rolly would make up an answer if he didn't know the actual one! He was charming and full of charisma. He was, well, full of it!

- **A kid at heart.** All of the nieces and nephews fondly remember how Uncle Rolly would get down on the floor and play with them. He had a unique ability to enter a child's world and develop a rapport with them.

- **A fan of the CU Buffaloes.** No more need be said!

- **A private individual.** As outgoing as Rolly was, he kept his own counsel and was a very private person, and was at times even aloof. In an article in the September 11, 1976 *Denver Post,* the headline reads "He Loves Being Up Creek" with the sub-heading, "With a Paddle, That Is." The article begins. "For 'tranquillity', Roland Rautenstraus goes kayaking. The president of the University of Colorado likes to paddle peacefully around on a lake, a placid river or down an irrigation ditch in his maneuverable yellow kayak. It's big enough for two, but Rautenstraus, 51, prefers to go alone. 'Without being a grouch about it, I like to go off by myself for a while on Saturday or Sunday and enjoy seeing the fish and the muskrats and the birds without disturbing nature in any way,' he said." Rolly didn't talk deeply about himself with family. Not many of us do. But Willie said that the loss of his parents and his sister Ruth deeply affected him, and in the '80s, the family didn't see as much of him. Others noticed that he seemed to change during this time and would ask, "Have you seen or heard anything from Roland?" We knew that he frequently commuted to his condominium in East Vail. It was, I believe, a place where he could be with his own thoughts. To our great pleasure, in recent years, Rolly "came around" again to the family, and seemed to be more like his old self.

In addition to the collective family memories, we each had our own special relationship with Roland which produced impressions and stories. Regarding my aunt and uncle, there was always an affection between the two. Larry said that his mother Ruth related to him how, when courting, Rolly waited on the front porch of Willie's UNC sorority house and actively pursued her! To the family, Roland and Willie were always the "in" couple—so "with the times", so youthful and hip.

Willie, in every sense of the word, you were an equal partner to Rolly, and a definite asset to his career at the University of Colorado. You were truly a first lady in all respects. I know that you have many fond memories of Roland and your years together.

Curt also has wonderful memories of his dad. Here's a funny one. Curt remembers that Rolly was a big instigator in the CU Faculty/Student softball games. Rolly would pitch because he loved being the center of attention. He was also the score keeper! How did Rolly keep score? He would hold up the grade book, and naturally, the students would let him win!

And here is a poignant remembrance of Curt's. Many of us knew that Rolly was afraid of flying. There was an episode during World War II involving an airplane that terribly affected him. The first time that Rolly flew again, after some 30 years, was to make it back in time for his son's birthday.

Larry Dumler is the oldest nephew. His memories of his uncle date back to Roland coming home from the war and staying with his parents on 38th Avenue in Wheat Ridge. He and Susan remember Rolly and Willie visiting them in Oregon in the mid 1960s at the time of the Alaskan earthquake. The road to Ecola State Park was washed out, but Larry knew a jeep trail, and he shuttled them in. They had the park to themselves for a picnic!

In 1967, Sue and Larry stayed with Rolly and Willie for a while and remember that they helped them look for a house. They fondly remember dinners at Colaccis in Louisville, and how much Rolly loved the Rose wine! They recall Rolly's 50th birthday party at Ken and Betty Bangs'; attending CU football games together; snowmobiling with both Roland and Willie; and the fun-loving Uncle Roland who played with their four girls.

Larry shared that Roland's students often told him that Raut was the finest teacher they ever had. In a *Denver Post* article from March of 1979 that talks about Rolly's impending retirement as president of CU, the then-president of the Boulder Student Union, Dan Caplis (who incidentally is now a prominent attorney and television commentator) is quoted as saying, "He [Roland] has been available, accessible, straightforward always . . . We could call and he would return the call within a few hours . . . Even students who weren't involved in student government could get in to see him. Just students who wanted to talk to him about something. And the students who worked with him just loved him. I don't know how they'll replace him."

My sister Diane remembers Roland and Willie's generosity. "They always gave me something out-of-the-ordinary that my parents couldn't afford," she said, recalling a beaded purse and a fur hat as two memorable gifts. Another example of their incredible generosity was hosting her wedding in November, 1972. They opened up their house and paid for everything from the chairs to the champagne as a wedding present.

She recalls that he loved the Christmas song "What Child is This?" She remembers how interested Rolly was in her attending college, and how he made a special trip to Wheat Ridge to talk to her about it upon her graduation from high school in 1967. Another tender memory was in 1981, shortly after her husband died, when Rolly reached out to her by inviting her and me up to Vail to spend the day with him.

I have many great Rolly stories and memories. Roland and Willie were my godparents. I remember Rolly agreeing to be the auctioneer at two of my backyard carnivals benefiting the Muscular Dystrophy Association. He could sell anything—and did!

Rolly knew I was interested in politics and the presidency. I was so thrilled when he gave me a letter that he had received from President-elect Richard Nixon in 1968 asking him to recommend individuals to his new administration. I still have the letter.

I remember in 1976 deciding against attending CU because Rolly was the president. I didn't want any expectations preceding me. So I marched off to UNC at Greeley, and what happened on the first day? The professors asked, "Are you related to the Rautenstraus at CU?" I couldn't escape the name!

I remember coming home from college that first Thanksgiving. I couldn't wait to "rub it in" by giving Roly a UNC sweatshirt. He was so fun to kid! I also remember a time in my freshman year when Rolly and Willie invited me to have cocktails with them and the UNC and CSU presidents and their wives. I was beside myself!

I *barely* remember attending a certain CU football game, and visiting my aunt and uncle in their presidential box during half-time. Eddie Crowder was there, but I can't recall any other details. I had drunk too much with my friends!

I remember as a reporter in Canon City seeing Rolly's CU commencement address on Page One of the local daily paper, and swelling with pride. I remember vividly the time that Rolly gave me a private tour of the CU campus and his huge office. He seemed so comfortable and laid back in the role of president.

I remember how he always hummed the first line of a favorite song, " 'Twas a portrait of Jenny". He loved that song. I remember meeting Governor Romer at the governor's mansion and after introducing myself, he said, "Are you related to Roland?" I can't tell you how proud I was of him and of the Rautenstraus name.

More than anything, I will always remember Rolly's twinkle and smile.

The mystical poet Kahil Gibran, writing on death in his classic The *Prophet*, said "For what is it to die but to stand naked in the wind and to melt into the sun? And what is it to cease breathing, but to free the breath from its restless tides, that it may rise and expand and seek God unencumbered? Only when you drink from the river of silence shall you indeed sing. And when you have reached the mountain top, then you shall begin to climb. And when the earth shall claim your limbs, then shall you truly dance."

I am not sure what Uncle Rolly is doing now. Here's something he once said about retirement, "There are several things I know I *won't* do. I will not be president elsewhere. If I were to stay, I would stay here. I know that if I went someplace else, for the first few weeks, the people would be different and very exciting. Then my tomorrows would be just like my yesterdays."

Once, nearing the end of his CU presidency, he was asked about his plans for the future. "I've never done anything I prized as much or felt as privileged to do, but if there is any consciousness of overstaying my welcome, I think this is a good time to go," he said, adding, "You never really control your own destiny completely. But I hope to continue to meet with individuals very much for the purpose of knowing what they are aspiring to, what they think is happening . . ."

Rolly didn't overstay his welcome, but I guess it was his time to move on. Perhaps he's teaching somewhere, somehow. Definitely, he's holding court, and loving every moment of it!

The measure of life, after all, is not its duration, but its donation. What a donation Uncle Rolly made in my life—and the lives of everyone here.

This says it best for me: "May you be lucky enough to remember a friend it hurts so much to lose, yet whose every memory fills you with such joy that no pain on earth could have made you miss the experience."

Rolly, I speak for everyone here. We wouldn't have missed the experience of you for anything! May God bless you.

MEMORIAL BY STEIN STURE (February 4, 1998)

"My Teacher, Friend and Fellow Department Faculty Member"

The University was the primary focus of Roland Rautenstraus' existence. It shaped him as a youth, matured him in middle age, and provided him with joy, reminiscence, and purpose in his later years.

Roland was one of 2,000 "V-12" Navy officer candidates who joined the 4,000 civilians on campus, and received their training at CU in the period 1942-1945. His aim was to become a civil engineer after leaving Colorado State College in Greeley and giving up on the idea of becoming a teacher. His father may have prevailed on him regarding the previous choice. Little did he know then that he would come full circle. Roland served in the Pacific with two of his roommates from CU—Karl Pister and Stephen Bechtel.

He returned to CU in 1945 to complete his BS in civil engineering—he had just one semester's worth of work remaining to get his degree. The Dean of Engineering, Clarence Eckel, agreed to his plan of study with the condition that Raut help teach for one year. The permanent or regular faculty then was only 12, and the Department was swamped with over 500 students, most of them returning veterans like him. Roland agreed to teach for one year. He stayed for 52. As he completed his undergraduate degree, he also played football. He had a marvelous time and was at the start of a fruitful academic career. His father was a theologian and Roland related that his dad took modest offense when Raut characterized the academy and this institution in particular as his temple.

Over the years, Roland taught statics, surveying, geodesy, photogrammetry, city planning, transportation engineering, construction materials, methods and management, and engineering contracts. He taught mostly at the undergraduate level, and usually to large classes. In the period 1959-1964, he was the first Department chair. All his predecessors had been Heads.

After this, he rose through the ranks (as we have heard) and served in several University administrative positions, finally as president, between 1974 and January 1980. While he was in administration for over 20 years, he managed somehow to stay close to teaching. I took a city planning course from him 28 years ago. Charles Hallenbeck was the intended instructor, but Raut ended up teaching much of the class. We students were pleasantly amazed having the vice president as teacher. Professor Rautenstraus had a wonderful ability to communicate both the big picture and the essentials. We were impressed by his insight, wisdom and good humor. He was an inspiration to all of us.

One of the many things I recall from the class is that he related that he was not fond of air transportation. Personally, he avoided flying, he said, due to an incident he had been part of many years ago. When he traveled, he preferred to go by car. He did not say more about that. Many years later, I learned an incredible story from his former classmate, Karl Pister, former Dean of Engineering at University of California, Berkeley and Chancellor Emeritus at University of California, Santa Cruz, that in 1944, Raut and several others had been on a supply mission someplace in the Pacific, and Raut's harness had somehow been caught while the cargo dropped. As the story goes, he ended up being dragged through the air after the airplane for some time. Then, the plane developed engine trouble. They managed to drag Roland indoors just minutes before the plane ditched. No wonder he had had enough of flying.

Roland was always a wonderful storyteller, but he did not say much about his personal adventures, especially the scary ones. He tended to dwell on the more agreeable and pleasant parts of his experiences.

After serving as president, Roland came back to the Department and assumed a full teaching load. He immediately established himself among our best teachers—for many years, perhaps, the best instructor of large classes. The larger his classes, the better the course and instructor ratings were. In fact, his ratings were almost entirely As for the past 17 years. Roland always came to work early, and for over a decade he started our department coffee pot.

He taught every semester, including summers. His teaching was characterized by relevance to real problems. Roland was always enthusiastic about his work and always well informed. Teaching and service were his strengths. He did not engage in research of the kind we presently do.

While his colleagues often lamented on the preparation of our students, Roland did not. He would say, "The students are just the same now as they were years ago, perhaps even better. They know so much now. My generation was rather naive and uninformed in comparison." On student behavior, he often reflected on how different the students are now compared to 30 years ago, during the height of the Vietnam era, when he, on occasion, was asked by President and Mrs. Smiley to camp out by their entrance door to deal with any irate students that might attack during the night. Students held stronger views then, but were less civil.

Through all his activities, we saw a skilled and curious intelligence at work. Roland's lecture style was brilliant. His lectures were notable for their grace and clarity, and his ability to capture the attention of his audience left them with the feeling that they shared his understanding of the subject. He guided his students in so gentle and appealing a manner that he did not intimidate or silence them. He encouraged the students to back up their general assertions with specific evidence. Roland was always concerned about the student's intellectual development and well being.

He treated his students with great respect, which in his eyes included holding them to high standards, and closely followed their careers as long as he lived, helping them find good positions, critiquing their papers and work. No wonder he was so widely admired, professionally and personally. A few years ago, he remarked that he is now starting to have the "grandchildren of his former students in his classes." We miss him for the energy and enthusiasm he brought to the classroom, for his warmth and accessibility, and for his ability to create in the classroom an atmosphere in which the students felt invited to participate in discussions.

Roland was a person of many exceptional talents which he used with great effect. He was a dedicated servant of the University. He had a strong sense of duty and fairness and what is right. He was an excellent judge of character. Raut's ready wit and unfailing loyalty to the University and his friends are among the traits that make him deeply missed.

He compiled an impressive array of service both at the national level and internationally, ranging from consultations to Nissan Motors, membership on the North-Central University Accreditation

Board, and advisor to the Board of Visitors at Georgia Tech. His civic and community activities were extensive.

Roland was always a cheerful man. He avoided self-pity. He was not for high drama in discussions: "If you need drama, read Shakespeare," he would say. He also had a strong sense of history and was often philosophical. He thought it was the obligation of the living to dedicate themselves to the unfinished work of those who had gone before. In this age of changing educational paradigms, he maintained that there is no substitute for good lecturing and effective use of the chalkboard.

Roland succeeded in passing the only test that matters: he has given back to the world more than he has taken out of it. His lasting legacy is his work as an outstanding civil engineering educator and a shaper of the University and an example and mentor to faculty and students alike.

Roland was a social being of charm and wit, who felt that missing a party was a great sin.

We had the ridiculous notion that he would beat the odds, and go on for a hundred more years. We could really use his teaching. We are grieving for the friend and colleague we knew and dearly admired.

"Aufwiedersehn, Roland." We miss you!

MEMORIAL BY KURT GERSTLE (February 4, 1998)

"Raut: My Friend and Colleague"

Raut stood at a turning point in the life of our University at a time when it changed from a sturdy little provincial school—albeit with people who were giants of their time—to a world-open, world-known university.

Let me share this turning point with you through the narrow view of Raut's department at that time: civil engineering. Prior to Raut's time—the early post-WW II years—we had an old testament hierarchy: a small, locally-bred faculty, deeply rooted in the turn of the century (the last century, that is); an authoritarian, if grandfatherly, department head, with tenure limited only by retirement; a vision bounded by the State of Colorado's borders.

A plain-spoken, plain-thinking, hard-working, honorable system which produced capable professionals well-rooted in the past, but unaware of changes lurking in the future: a society increasingly dependent on engineering know-how, computers, environmental problems, space travel, telecommunications. All this called for a more creative approach.

Raut became department chairman at just that turning point. In fact, his was the first chairmanship in the department, characterized by a limited term of elected office and greater responsiveness to faculty concerns. It was a democratic regime that was a symptom an academic revolution. And Raut was at its head. The department was growing in size, in stature, in world view. Raut was at the forefront of the struggle for a forward-looking department aware of our society's problems, groping for solutions. Faculty came who brought with them the idea that a university should be involved not only with the propagation, but also the creation of knowledge. Graduate study and research found its place alongside established activities.

Now, much of this is accepted and expected. The early struggles, and those who fought them, are forgotten. But let us remember that the man whom we honor here was deeply involved in shaping the university which we know now. He was successful and went on to higher places and higher honors. Others will talk about that, but let us remember where it all started.

APPENDIX B

THE THREE-POWER PACT

Three young, junior-high boys—in the mid-1930s—felt compelled to enter into an oath they called "The Three-Power Non-Agression Pact" (sic) to pledge their concurrence of how they should behave. The pact reads: "I, a member of the Pact, do hereby solemly (sic) swear hereafter not to yell or cast deregetory (sic) remarks at any girls which might prove embarrassing to any of the signers of the Pact."

The signers of the pact were (in order of signature): Rolland Rautenstraus, Bud Smith and Bob Joseph Dole. The hand-written document has no date but bears the seal of the local Lutheran Church in Russell, Kansas. (Note: Roland was spelling his name with two "l"s at this time. Raut, who in his adult years prided himself on being an expert "wordsmith," would be amused at the spelling and grammar of his youth.)

RESUME OF RAUTENTRAUS

ROLAND CURT RAUTENSTRAUS

BIRTHDATE February 27, 1924, Gothenburg, Nebraska

DEATH December 25, 1997, Boulder, Colorado

MARRIED Willie Atler, June 30, 1946

CHILDREN Curt Dean, October 22, 1947

EDUCATION University of Colorado, B.S.
(Civil Engineering), 1946

University of Colorado, M.S., 1949

University of New Mexico, Doctor of Laws,
honoris causa, 1976

ARMED SERVICE EXPERIENCE
Lt. (jg) Civil Engineer Corps., USNR, 1942-46

TEACHING EXPERIENCE
Instructor (part-time), University of Colorado, 1946-47
Instructor, University of Colorado, 1947-50
Assistant Professor, University of Colorado, 1950-54
Associate Professor, University of Colorado, 1954-57
Professor, University of Colorado, 1957-1993
Chairman, Department of Civil Engineering, University of
Colorado, 1959-64
Associate Dean of the Faculties of the University of Colorado,
1964-68
Vice President for Educational and Student Relations,
University of Colorado, 1968-70

Vice President for University Relations, University of
    Colorado, 1970-73
Executive Vice President, University of Colorado, 1973-74
President, University of Colorado, June 1, 1974 -
    January 15, 1980
President Emeritus and Professor Emeritus, 1993-97

PROFESSIONAL EXPERIENCE
McNeil Engineers, San Diego, California and Lesser I. Mahoney
    Architects and Engineers, Phoenix, Arizona - one year
U.S. Navy Civil Engineer Corps., USNR, 1942-46
Summer 1950 - Surveys in Colorado and Utah including
    Humphries Phosphate Company, Vernal, Utah
Summer 1952 - Consultant for the Topographic Branch of the
    United States Geological Survey, Denver, Colorado
Summer 1957 - Consultant for Ken R. White Engineering
    Company, Denver
Summers 1958-59-60 - Consultant for several governmental
    agencies and private companies including Hartzel Engineering
    Company, Frank Drexel, Inc., Colorado Department of
    Highways, U.S. Department of Health, Education and Welfare
Licensed as Land Surveyor State of Colorado
Licensed as a registered professional engineer, State of Colorado,
    1955-97
Consultant for Travelers Insurance Company, 1958-59
Educational Panel for Esso Refining Humble Oil Company, 1960
Board of Directors, Northwest Engineering Company, 1969-97
Consultant to States of New York, California, Texas, Hawaii,
    Illinois, etc., on High-Tech Transfer, 1982-86
Consultant, States of Ohio, California, Georgia, 1990-1995

SPECIAL TEACHING PROGRAMS AND INSTITUTES
Summer 1956 - Director of special school for the Colorado
    Department of Highways.
      This four-week program was established for the Colorado
    Department of Highways as an instructional program for
    selected individuals of the Colorado Department of Highways
    for upgrading capabilities as civil engineers.
Summer 1958 - Director of special school for the Colorado De-
    partment of Highways.
      This program was an instructional program established for
    the purpose of upgrading personnel of the Colorado
    Department of Highways to the position of party chief.

Director - Annual Colorado Highway Engineering Conference,
    1958-61
Summer 1961 - General Chairman National Annual Conference,
    the Prestressed Concrete Institute
Director - Graduate Institute of Foreign Highway Engineers,
    Summer 1963. This was a nine-week program for training high-
    way engineers from nine nations under the financial
    support of the U.S. Bureau of Public Roads and the agency for
    International Development.
General Chairmen of the Third International Conference on
    Electronic Computation, sponsored by the American Society
    of Civil Engineers and the Division of Structural Mechanics, 1963.
Summer 1964 - Jury for Awards, National Competition for the
    Lincoln Arc Welding Foundation.

RESEARCH PROJECTS
Director - Research projects sponsored by Wallace Tierman Prod-
    ucts Company on uses of aneroid barometers, 1950-52
Consultant - Army Ordinance Contract Project on Thin Web
    Members, 1955
Director - Project on Aggregate Treatment Studies sponsored by
    the Colorado Department of Highways and the U.S. Bureau of
    Public Roads, 1962-64
Co-Director - Broadway Study.
    This was a sponsored research project of the Colorado
    Department of Highways and the U.S. Bureau of Public Roads
    to determine the behavioral characteristics of arterial streets.
Consultant for the U.S. Department of State on Higher Education
    Program in Africa, 1977

CIVIC AND COMMUNITY ACTIVITIES
Member of City of Boulder Planning Board, 1952-58
Member of Inter-Regional Planning Board on Annexation, 1957
City of Boulder Water Board, 1957-60
Colorado Council on Arts and Humanities, 1967-73
Board of Directors, YMCA, 1971-73
Governor's Energy Task Force, 1973-74
Colorado State Bonding Authority, 1984-97
Denver Center for the Performing Arts
Member of Board of Directors, Rocky Mountain Writers Guild
United Way Campaign Leadership Team
Director, Radio Station KCFR
Director, Colorado Public Radio Network

HONORS AND CITATIONS
Faculty Appreciation Award, Associated Engineering Students, 1963
Faculty Appreciation Award for Outstanding Teaching, 1964
Member Chi Epsilon, National Civil Engineering Honorary Fraternity
Member Tau Beta Pi, National Engineering Honorary Fraternity
Listed, American Men of Science
Listed, Who's Who in America
Awarded Bronze Medal, Lincoln Arc Welding Foundation
Awarded Robert L. Stearns Award, 1965
Awarded Norlin Medal, Alumni Recognition Award, 1974
University of Northern Colorado Alumni Association, Columbine Award, 1975
Distinguished Engineering Alumnus Award, College of Engineering, Univ.of Colo., 1975
Rocky Mountain Center on Environment Award, 1976-77
Alfred J. Ryan Award by Professional Engineers of Colorado, 1977
Consulting Engineers Council of Colorado Award, June 1979
University Gold Medal, 1979
Centennial Medal, College of Engineering, University of Colorado, 1993
General Palmer Award, American Consulting Engineers of Colorado, 1996
Department of Civil Engineering Award for Outstanding Contribution
Student Award for Outstanding Teaching
University of Colorado Athletic Hall of Fame

PRINCIPAL PROFESSIONAL SOCIETY MEMBERSHIPS
Member, American Society Photogrammetry
Member, American Society for Engineering Education
Member, American Society of Civil Engineers
Member, NASULGC Committee on Voluntary Support, Washington, DC - one year term
Chairman, National Committee on Surveying and Mapping of American Society for Engineering Education
Chairman, National Sub-Committee of American Society for Engineering Education on Surveying for Non-Civil Engineering Students
Member, National Committee on Educational Policy of the American Society of Photogrammetry

Member, National Committee on Accreditation of Colleges of
Engineering for the Engineers Council for Professional
Development
Chairman, Association of the Western States Chairman of Civil
Engineering Departments
Served on committee of 40 engineering educators for study of na-
tional engineering education sponsored by the National Sci-
ence Foundation
Member, North Central Accrediting Program
Chairman, Committee 8 American Society for Engineering
Education
Member, Council Presidents of Western Regional Scientific
Laboratories, University of New   Mexico, Albuquerque,
New Mexico, 1976-97
Vice Chairman Universities Research Association, Washington,
D.C., Organization of Council Presidents and ex-officio
member Executive Committee, 1977-97
Association of American Universities, Washington, D.C.,
Committee on the Organization of Federal Educational
Programs, 1977-97
Members Representative, University Corporation for Atmospheric
Research, Boulder, Colorado, 1977
Member, IIE, Institute of International Education, Denver,
Colorado, 1977-97
Chairman, Council of Presidents and Chairman of the Executive
Committee, URA, 1978-79
Chief Executive Officer representing Big 8 Conference as a
member of ad hoc committee Title IX, 1978-97
Board of Editorial Contributors, Rocky Mountain News, 1979-97
Board of Directors, Denver Educational Entry to Energy Programs,
1979-97
Member, Colorado Supreme Court Council Judicial Performance
Committee, State of Colorado, Denver, Colorado, 1979-97

PRINCIPAL PROFESSIONAL TALKS AND PAPERS
VALUE OF SURVEYING presented at third National Surveying
Teachers Conference, 1952
ADVANCED METHODS OF FIELD ENGINEERING presented at the
29th Annual Colorado Highway Conference, 1956
TRENDS IN ENGINEERING EDUCATION, 45th Annual Conven-
tion, Colorado Society of Engineers, 1961
A COMPREHENSIVE PLAN, Conference for Planning Officials,
1958

URBAN PLANNING, Colorado City Managers Institute, 1959

CHANGING TRENDS IN ENGINEERING EDUCATION, 45th
Annual Convention Colorado Society of Engineers, 1961

ENGINEERING ENROLLMENTS, Engineering Manpower Conference, 1961

CHANGING CURRICULUM presented to the National Meeting
for the American Society of Engineering Education at
Lexington, KY, 1961

NEW DESIGNS, 7th Annual Prestressed Concrete Institute, 1961

LAND USE, 11th Building Industry Congress, 1962

ACQUISITION, URBAN AREA BASE MAPS, Institute of City
Engineers, 1962

PLANNING CLINIC presented at the 4th Annual Institute for
Planning Officials, 1962

CONTROLLED ACCESS HIGHWAYS, 35th Annual Colorado
Highway Conference, 1962

GENERAL PLANNING FOR MUNICIPAL STREET SYSTEMS,
Institute for City Engineers, 1963

NEW TRENDS ENGINEERING EDUCATION, Regional Meeting
American Society of Civil Engineers, 1963

LAND SURVEYING LAWS presented at the national meeting of
the American Society of Photogrammetry

WHY ENTER ENGINEERING, Annual Building Industry
Conference, 1963

MAN AND THE URBAN PLAN presented at Professional Engineers
Conference, 1961

PHOTOGRAMMETRY: A GEOLOGIST'S TOOL, Colorado
Scientific Society

ENGINEERING MEASUREMENTS, paper presented at National
meeting of the American Society for Engineering Education,
1962

TRANSPORTATION CURRICULUM presented at University of
Illinois, 1966

BUILDING BRIDGES TO MEET THE STRESS OF THE SEVENTIES
presented to the American Alumni Council, Juarez, Mexico,
1972

AMERICAN HIGHER EDUCATION IN THE SEVENTIES AND THE
ROLE OF ALUMNI AFFAIRS ADMINISTRATORS presented to
Alumni Administration Institute of American Alumni Council,
Snowmass-Aspen, CO, 1972

EVALUATING YOUR ALUMNI PROGRAM IN DOLLARS THAT
MAKE SENSE presented at the American Alumni Council
Tri-District Conference, Phoenix, AZ, 1973

ALUMNI AND DEVELOPMENT-A PARTNERSHIP presented at the
American Alumni Council National Conference, Vancouver,
B.C., Canada, 1973

ALUMNI ASSOCIATION OBJECTIVES IN RELATION TO
UNIVERSITY OBJECTIVES IN THE NEXT DECADE, presented
at the Advanced Institute in Alumni Administration of the
American Alumni Council, Snowmass-Aspen, CO, 1973

HIGHER EDUCATION IN THE UNITED STATES - THIRTY YEARS
OF CRISIS, presented to the Consulting Engineers Council, CO,
1975

FRATERNITIES AND THE FUTURE, presented at the 134th Annual
Chi Psi Fraternity Convention, 1975

SYMPOSIUM ON NUCLEAR AND PUBLIC HEALTH AND
WELFARE IN COLORADO, presented at the Nuclear Energy
and Public Health and Welfare Symposium, 1975

AMERICAN EDUCATION ON TRIAL AND TEST, presented to the
annual joint convention of the Colorado Association of School
Boards and the Department of General Administrators of the
Colorado Association of School Executives, 1975

THE ENGINEER AND EDUCATION, presented to the
Metropolitan Chapter of the Professional Engineers of
Colorado, 1975

COPING WITH THE FISCAL CRISES IN HIGHER EDUCATION,
presented at the annual meeting of the North Central
Conference, Summer Schools, Chicago, 1976

PEOPLE GO FOR PEOPLE, presented at annual meeting of the
Young Men's Christian Association of Metropolitan Denver, 1976

THE UNIVERSITY OF COLORADO CENTENNIAL, presented at the
open house reception at the Auraria Learning Resources
Center, Denver, Colorado, 1976

CONSUMERISM IN THE WORLD OF HIGHER EDUCATION,
presented at Conference of the National Association of Student
Personnel Administrators, Denver, 1976

HIGHER EDUCATION IN THE UNITED STATES: DECADES OF
CRISIS, presented to the Kiwanis Club, Greeley, CO, 1976

AFFIRMATIVE ACTION: MYTH VS. REALITY, presented at the
Conference for Governing Board Members and College
Administrators, Colorado Springs, 1976

PROJECTS FOR LEADERSHIP ON CAMPUS, presented at the
Mid-Year Seminar Program of the ACE Fellows Program in Academic Administration of the Office of Leadership Development
in Higher Education of the American Council on Education,
Boulder, CO, 1977

IS HIGHER EDUCATION WORTH IT?, presented to the Denver
Mile High Optimist Club, Denver, CO, 1977
TRAFFIC SAFETY IN THE MID 1970s, presented to the Colorado
Safety Association, Denver, CO, 1977
IS MANAGING HIGHER EDUCATION WORTH IT?, presented to
the Colorado Safety Association, Denver, CO, 1977
ANNUAL MEETING OF PROFESSIONAL ENGINEERS OF
COLORADO, Boulder, 1977
VAIL SYMPOSIUM/SEVEN, Vail, CO, 1977
LAKEWOOD CHAMBER OF COMMERCE, Lakewood, CO, 1978
NATIONAL ASSOCIATION OF ACCOUNTANTS, Denver, CO,
1978
A SYMPOSIUM ON MEXICO-UNITED STATES ECONOMIC RELA-
TIONS, Boulder, CO, 1978
HIGHER EDUCATION IN THE ROCKIES, Keystone, CO, 1979
EVANS SCHOLARS, Denver, CO, 1979
SAVINGS AND LOAN LEAGUE OF COLORADO, Denver, CO, 1979
PUBLIC ACCOUNTANTS SOCIETY OF COLORADO, Silverthorne,
CO, 1979
NINTH ANNUAL INVITATIONAL CONFERENCE FOR REGIONAL
CAMPUS ADMINISTRATORS, Colorado Springs, CO, 1979
THE AMERICAN SOCIETY OF AGRONOMY, Ft. Collins, CO, 1979
KEYNOTE ADDRESS: Colorado Highway Engineer Conference,
1993

PRINCIPAL PUBLICATIONS
PHOTOGRAMMETRY, Engineers Bulletin, 1951
THE VALUE OF SURVEYING, published in the proceedings of the
3rd Annual Meeting of Committee 8 American Society of
Education, 1953
FIELD PROBLEMS FOR PLANE SURVEYING, with R. E. Rathburn,
published at the   University of Colorado, 1954
SURVEYING AND MAPPING, co-author C.V. Hallenbeck,
published at the University of Colorado, 1957
SURVEYING IN THE ENGINEERING CURRICULUM presented at
the Annual Meeting of the American Society of Engineering
Education, published 1960
GIVE ME A TARGET, Civil Engineering Proceedings of the
American Society of Civil Engineers, 1961
ENGINEERING ENROLLMENTS, published in proceedings of
President's Manpower Conference, 1961
URBAN PLANNING, published in the manual on Urban
Planning for Environmental Health, 1962

ENGINEERING STUDY REPORT, contributor with other partici-
pants in Journal of Engineering Education, 1962

AGGREGATE TREATMENT STUDY, a research report distributed
by Highway Research Board, Washington, D.C., 1963

STREET SYSTEMS, Colorado Municipalities, Volume 39, #5, 1963

STREET SYSTEMS IN URBAN PLANNING, Colorado
Municipalities, 1963

BROADWAY STUDY, co-author C.V. Hallenbeck, a research report,
University of Colorado and U.S. Bureau of Public Roads, 1964

RESEARCH AT EDUCATIONAL INSTITUTIONS, published in Vital
Speeches of The Day, Vol. XLV, #7, June 15, 1979

GUEST EDITORIAL: THE ENGINEER AS ADVOCATE, Journal of
the Society for Experimental Stress Analysis, Vol. 19, #9,
September 1979

AGRONOMY - SOLVING PROBLEMS, A.S.A. Special Publication,
#37, American Society of Agronomy, August 1980, 15 pp.

VARIOUS RESEARCH REPORTS SUBMITTED BY NCHEMS to states
involving the interrelationship of high technology and higher
education, 1982-86

VARIOUS ACCREDITATION REPORTS for the North Central
Association involving institutions of higher education, 1980-97

PRIMARY ACTIVITIES SINCE RETIREMENT (1993 - 1997)

Committees and Public Service

Member of Executive Committee of Colorado Public Radio and a
member of its Board of Directors. Raised funding and responsible for
two new stations in Vail, Colorado and
Pueblo, Colorado.

Member of Colorado Post-Secondary Education Funding Authority. This state board aids in financing post-secondary education
physical facilities and cultural facilities in the state. Participated in
the funding of approximately 100 million dollars of facilities. Membership on this board was by Governor's appointment with the
consent of the Colorado Senate.

Teaching

Taught an average of one course per term. Those courses tended to
be required under-graduate courses of relatively large enrollments.

Consulting

Extensive consultations with Strategic Initiatives of Washington, DC and the National Center for Higher Educational Management Systems of Boulder, Colorado. These projects involved educational policy, technology transfer, and work on engineering projects. Projects resulted in written reports and formulation of recommendations. A partial list of projects included:

1. Work for State of Ohio in evaluating the needs of technical education in the Dayton, Ohio region, particularly related to the needs of the Air Force Laboratories associated with Wright Patterson Field.

2. An extensive series of studies for proposed revisions in the Accounting Programs for the American Association of Accountants. This project involved reviewing all existing programs of accounting in the U.S.A. and interviewing a number of leaders in the field, both in universities and in practice.

3. A series of projects for the Georgia Institute of Technology, reviewing their process of distribution of funding to various programs and to determine the extent to which the allocation were cost-effective.

4. Consulting work relating to future development in the United States by the Nissan Corporation involving projects dealing with sponsoring research, funding educational programs, plant locations, and governmental relations.

5. Various and sundry speeches to schools, and to local groups, as well as to groups throughout the U.S. and abroad.

SELECTION OF SPEECHES BY RAUTENSTRAUS

The American Society of Agronomy
National Convention, August 7, 1979
Student Center, CSU, Fort Collins, CO

It is an honor and a pleasure to be with you today.

I think it can fairly be said that as American Agricultural Scientists, you represent the single most successful on-going scientific inquiry in the history of civilization.

I can think of no other group of investigators who can appropriately claim to have worked more profound, sweeping, and lasting changes on the way men and women live than can American Agronomists.

Indeed, you have been so successful that the American people have awarded you the highest accolade our civilization is capable of bestowing. That is to say, they take you for granted.

The fact of the matter is that American agricultural science has so thoroughly reshaped the world that it is impossible to conceive of an ordering of modern civilization that is not underpinned by its contributions.

In this regard, I think it is significant that not long ago reports began appearing in the financial press to the effect that from India east through Asia and the Pacific basin, agricultural production is rising; birth rates and illiteracy rates are falling; per capita incomes are increasing; and the work of modernization is moving forward. The key, according to these reports, is agriculture. The Green Revolution, it seems, has taken hold and the signs are now unmistakable that a cycle of poverty, disease,and ignorance that is as old as

200

time is coming to an end.

This is a far different picture that the one painted at the beginning of the decade, when global famine was predicted for 1975—when many maintained that international development assistance should be allocated on the basis of a policy of "Triage" and governed by "Lifeboat Ethics"—and when the Green Revolution, that is to say the export of scientific agriculture to the less developed nations, was being loudly proclaimed a failure. Once again, it would appear, Reverend Malthus' moment has been deferred.

At first blush, this optimistic development might seem too good to be true—particularly at a time when everything in the world seems to be going wrong—but we really shouldn't be surprised by it. If history demonstrates anything, it is that a necessary precondition to the development of an industrial society is the emergence of a scientifically-based agriculture. As evidence of this, I think I can offer our own history as Exhibit A.

I think a strong case can be made for the proposition that the single most important piece of domestic legislation ever enacted by the Congress of the United States was the passage in 1866 of the Morrill Act. It assured the creation of a nationwide system of higher education designed to offer not the traditional, classical curriculum, but practical training in agriculture, science, technology, and education. Students were not only instructed in the application of science and technology to agriculture, but equally importantly, were trained to instruct others. As a result, within a generation—that is to say, by the beginning of the 20th Century—several profound changes had been set in motion.

First, American farming was well on the way to being put on a scientific footing, guaranteeing the nation an unequalled agricultural productivity that continues to this day. The advent of a scientific agriculture not only freed the country from the threat of famine and insured the population an ample diet, but it also made it possible to reach and exceed those goals without requiring that a disproportionately large share of the work force remain in agriculture.

Second, American industry had available to it a pool of scientists and engineers—and perhaps just as important: technicians, mechanics and machinists—that made possible the swift development and commercialization of the scientific discoveries of the day. It is hardly accidental that many innovations that were European in origin remained laboratory curiosities until America got hold of them. The attribution of this to the availability of American capital alone is not sufficient. Until the First World War, Europe's capital resources were considerably greater than our own.

Third, American primary and secondary education for the first time had available to it trained teachers in sufficient numbers to entertain seriously the notion of universal literacy. That, in turn, contributed significantly to turning the American worker into the most productive in the world during the first half of the 20th Century.

There are two points here that are worth stressing. First, scientific agriculture created the surpluses that made the swift industrialization of the republic possible. Second, the scientific processes that developed in an agricultural context had application in many other sectors of American life. One might call this "spin-off", but that is a wholly inadequate way of conveying the sense of it— somewhat like calling a prairie fire the spin-off of a match.

I think it is important to recall the historic contribution of agricultural science to our national development, because the value of science and research in American life is being questioned as it has not been questioned in a generation. It is certainly no secret that interest in and support for scientific inquiry is tending to decline in many quarters. Indeed, I think it is fair to say that scientific investigators generally are today encountering their most hostile reception since Sputnik. My sense of the matter is that research as it relates to agriculture has been somewhat immune until now—at least when compared to the antagonism experienced by workers in energy-related fields.

But it would be wishful thinking to assume this would last. Past public concern over the use of pesticides, chemical fertilizers, and feed additives, I suspect, will seem minor compared to what might be expected in the next few years as the advances in molecular biology and genetic engineering begin to move out of the laboratory and into the market. As the demands for a world free of risk become more insistent, I think it is incumbent on the scientific community to point to the potential of scientific inquiry as a balance for the exceptional emphasis that has been placed in recent years on the perils. This may well be the most urgent of scientist's public responsibilities.

In my estimation, the present hostility toward science and research stems from three sources—and I think it might be useful to discuss each briefly.

The first is a body of opinion that carried the concerns raised by the environmental movement beyond any rational criticism of the conduct of scientific and technological endeavors—to the point where all that remains is a distilled antipathy to science and technology in and of themselves. The influence of this neo-luddite school of thought has been far out of proportion to its numbers, but it has done much to poison the atmosphere in which the merits of scientific enterprises are debated.

At the very least, it has succeeded in shifting the burden of proof from those who oppose a national commitment to scientific inquiry to those who support it. Paradoxically, it has also tended to erode the credibility of the environmental movement to the point where its ability to participate in the national dialogue over scientific and technological policy is threatened.

The second source of hostility to scientific and technological progress derives from those parts of our society that have recoiled from the changes American life has experienced in the past two decades and who wish to return to the social ordering of an earlier time.

I do not think it is overstating the matter to say that the real cultural revolution of our time took place in the United States and not in China—and that it was fueled by advances in science and technology.

Such innovations as oral contraceptives, commercial jet aircraft, microprocessor-based computers, and satellite-based telecommunications-to say nothing of innovations in agriculture—altered the way Americans live. While a plurality may find such changes liberating, there will always be some who find them threatening—so perhaps it is not surprising that many who find their position in society in a state of protracted, traumatic, and unprecedented change should lash out at science. We may know intellectually that once technological genies are out of the bottle they are not put back into it—but that has never stopped people from trying.

The third group which has placed science under attack is politicians who want to make research a whipping boy for a whole range of frustrations and torments, which the political process has been unable to resolve. There is hardly any mystery to this. The best scape-goats are always those whose actions and conduct are not fully understood and, who for one reason or another, are not prepared to fight back. Politicians have traditionally understood far better than scientists that scientific progress does not proceed in a vacuum —and that the implications of scientific discoveries inevitably manifest themselves in the political life of the country—often as destabilizing influences. And, if there is one thing politicians hate, it is having to contend with factors whose behavior and consequences are neither understood nor predictable.

In this context, lately I've been musing about the life of George Boole, the father of Boolien Algebra, and I've concluded that perhaps it is better that he lived in the 19th Century rather than our own. No practical application was found for his abstract mathematical modeling until nearly a century after his death—at which time it was discovered that Boolien Algebra was uniquely suited for describing the behavior of electricity in computer circuits. Had Boole been working in our own age under a National Science Foundation Grant, Senator Proxmire would probably have given him the Golden Fleece Award.

It is not my intent to belabor all critics of American science and technology—indeed there is more than a little merit in many of the specific criticisms that have been raised. I think it is useful, however, to characterize the most serious sources of antagonism—because, in my estimation, it is the response to the present atmosphere of hostility that will determine the present social responsibilities of the scientist. Without in any way attempting to be comprehensive, I would like to suggest several specific responsibilities from which men and women of science are not free to desist.

First, the scientist must be the advocate of science. By this I do not mean that he or she must continually be making the case for more funding—although no great harm would accrue if the scientific community were less apologetic and bashful at budget time. Far more important, I think, is the need for scientists to become public advocates of the scientific method as the principal intellectual instrument of our civilization for solving problems. This may seem like a somewhat fatuous and gratuitous suggestion, but I can assure you it is not.

The fact of the matter is that there is a shocking ignorance in our society, not of the fruits of science and technology, but of the process of scientific inquiry, with the result that there is no real appreciation of what science can and cannot hope to accomplish. There is no doubt in my mind that a better public understanding of the scientific method—of science as a process rather than a product—would do more than any other single step to improve the climate in which science and technology function in the United States.

Second, the scientific community must improve its efficiency and productivity. This does not mean that scientists must subject themselves to speed up and time clocks in the laboratory, but it does mean it is incumbent upon them to approach the problem of resource allocation and project management with the same intelligence that is applied to the substance of the inquiry. Over two-thirds of the funding for American research comes from the public sector—and if there is one certainty in an uncertain world, it is that in an age of double-digit inflation, the public will not tolerate the management of 21st century projects with 19th century methods.

Third, the scientific community can no longer allow itself the luxury of assuming that everything it does is innately good and will be inherently well received. The hard fact is that it isn't and won't be. If scientific inquiry in America is to remain vital, its objectives must be continually examined, re-examined, justified, and explained—both to the public, and more importantly, to the scientific community itself. The value here is much the same as the value of zero-based budgeting. It is enormously useful to evaluate periodically one's own first premises and determine if they are still valid in the light of accumulated experience.

Fourth, the scientist has a social responsibility to think in terms of new ideas and not just refinements of old ones. I think this point, which seems obvious on the surface, needs emphasizing—because our society is becoming much less tolerant of error and much less willing to accept risk than has historically been the case. In such an atmosphere, the temptation is always there for the investigator to replow old fields rather than break new ground. It is a temptation that must be resisted decisively. The very essence of science lies in its ability to go beyond what is known—to find things that have never been found before, or build things that have never been built, or fashion concepts that have never been thought of. When it loses the ability to "create dangerously" in Camus' phrase, then its future is truly on the block.

Fifth, the scientist has a responsibility to be more open and candid with the public. The scientific community is not a priesthood. It has a responsibility—dictated by both intellectual honesty and morality—to explain what it is investigating, why particular inquiries are important, and how it is proceeding. I recognize that much of what is done in science is highly technical, but by the same token, I think the scientific community has consistently underestimated the ability of the public to comprehend technical information. I am convinced that a more open approach will result in a greater understanding and trust of science and a much greater appreciation of its potential.

Finally, I think the scientist has a public responsibility to share his vision with the world at large. Despite protests to the contrary, very little scientific research is undertaken exclusively for the pure love of knowing. The overwhelming majority of scientific investigations are undertaken in the expectation that they will ultimately contribute to the improvement of the human condition. In recent years, scientists have been very reluctant to share the vision of the future that is, in fact, the motivating force behind their exertions. I suspect it is because the scientific community is uncomfortable with the notion that a systematic and rational investigation may be undertaken for reasons that involve values that may ultimately be irrational.

I think an excellent example of this was the National Aeronautics and Space Administration's attempt to justify the Apollo project on the basis of its scientific by-products of "spin-off"—an exercise that was somewhat akin to justifying Columbus' discovery of America on the basis that the crew of the Santa Maria discovered some new ways to stow rope. In my estimation, the American people supported the Apollo project not because of spin-off and not out of desire to beat the Russians, but because it represented the realization of one of mankind's oldest dreams—the desire to visit another world and travel among the cosmos. It is a tragedy that NASA could not bring itself to affirm that dream in a public and non-apologetic manner. I suspect if it had, the space program would be enjoying much more support than it is today.

I guess what I am trying to say is that if the public responsibility of the scientist had to be distilled down to one word, that word would be "civilization." The scientific exercise cannot take place in isolation from the affairs of man—and it must be directed towards improving the human condition. As such, science is the embodiment of possibility—an affirmation of the proposition that human intelligence is still capable of solving human problems. Without that vision, without that sense of civilizing mission, science invariably becomes an elegant shell, devoid of real curiosity, innovation, or intellectual substance.

And if that happens, it will not be just science that will have lost, but the world will have lost as well.

PROFESSIONAL ENGINEERS OF COLORADO
Annual Meeting, June 10, 1977
The Harvest House, Denver, CO

I am particularly happy to be given this opportunity to discuss the prospects for engineering and education with you, although in the last fourteen years I have not been able to do much teaching in the College of Engineering or much engineering anywhere. Possibly your program chairman had the idea that my perspective on education from the lofty perch of general university administration enables me to see the forest better, regardless of whether I can see the trees. Sometimes I think that vantage point just keeps me more generally confused. But with this disclaimer quickly out of the way, let me say I welcome this opportunity to mingle with you professionals, and it's a special pleasure to find some of my former civil engineering students among you.

As an alumnus of engineering education, I can't help but note that the wayward course of my own career illustrates the fact that this kind of academic preparation has relevance for a variety of occupational avenues. To view that preparation as having benefit exclusively for those individuals who choose to enter engineering is to undersell the discipline. It has a long tradition of training people in the processes of decision making. In fact, those processes are inherent in the mode of engineering instruction. And the habits of mind they inculcate are of great value for people in a lot of vocations not directly related to engineering.

So much by way of preface.

I would like to suggest to you today that both higher education and the engineering profession share two common problems. The first is the fiscal constraints imposed by persistent inflation and an uncertain economic recovery. The other, and perhaps more serious, is a crisis of public confidence.

I am sure I'm giving away no secrets when I tell you universities are suffering a fiscal squeeze the likes of which they have never experienced before. While expenses have been soaring, traditional sources of revenue—state government appropriations, federal grants, and endowment income—have been falling in counterpoint to the rising costs.

If there is one group before whom this point need not be belabored, it is this one. The engineering profession has, if anything, felt the sting of inflation and fiscal constraints more sharply than the academy. In this regard, I am struck by two reports which appeared in last week's papers. On the same day it was reported that workmen on the Alaska Pipeline completed the final weld; it was also announced that the final construction costs might well be in excess of $9 billion, or over 1,000 percent of the $900 million 1969 estimate.

In the lower 48, I doubt if there is a single state which is not scrambling for highway maintenance funds, let alone monies for new projects, some of which are years overdue. And the fact that the President of the United States would attempt to audit the hitherto sacrosanct contents of the Congressional pork barrel and cast out dozens of reclamation projects—an act of political daring which must rank next to Evel Knievel's abortive attempt to leap over a swimming pool of sharks—suggests that the present fiscal crisis runs far deeper than we would like to believe.

I would like to suggest, however, that the financial constraints afflicting both higher education and engineering stem from more than just the occurrence of inflationary peaks at a time when the economy has dipped into unsuspected valleys. I suspect that a second—and in all likelihood more serious cause—is a loss of public confidence in both higher technology and higher education. To put it bluntly, people no longer think we can get the job done.

In education, the trend has been evident for some years. An all-consuming interest in this once-hollowed institution seems simply to have disappeared. It is no longer seen as providing an opportunity which should be granted by a democratic society. The collegiate experience has lost its charm as a symbol of superior status, as fertile soil for mate selection, as a guarantor of a professional career, and even as the most respected repository of human knowledge. This disenchantment has inevitably raised doubts about the wisdom of continued heavy public or private investment in education beyond the high school.

For engineering, public questioning began over the relationship between the environment and technological development. You know the essentials of the evolution of issue. In the earlier years of our national growth, it is certainly clear now, we were inordinately preoccupied with the exploitation of our natural resources and the wholesale destruction of our wildlife when any economic gain was involved. And our technological revolution went on its merry and marvelous way with little or no attention to any possible injurious effect. By the mid-1960's, we became sufficiently conscience-stricken and alarmed to go overboard in the opposite direction. We pressed our environmental concerns to the point where we did real damage to our economy and our standard of living. In the past few years, we've come to learn—intellectually at least—that we cannot have both a dynamic economy and a Garden of Eden, that the gains in one are rarely won without some expense to the other. But matters have not stopped here.

About the time that we were realizing the limits of environmentalism, the sheiks of the Persian Gulf reminded us of the limits of technology. Although predictions of an energy crisis began as early as 1972, it wasn't until the Arab oil embargo of late 1973 that the magnitude and the seriousness of the problem intruded on the public's consciousness.

That was nearly four years ago. Since then, there have been a multitude of solutions proposed, ranging from thermonuclear to solar to wind—in short, from science fiction, to 'doing it with mirrors,' to reinventing the wheel. But—despite the talk of 'space programs,' of 'Manhattan projects,' of crash efforts—very little has been forthcoming, at least insofar as the public can perceive.

I submit to you that the reason the President's energy program, with its emphasis on conservation, has been quietly accepted by the majority of the American people is that large numbers of Americans have despaired of seeing the problem solved by either increasing supplies or putting alternative energy sources on line—at least within their lifetimes.

This development has led to an even more disturbing one: the growing number of citizens who have come to discount the value of technology in sustaining the quality of life, or who have concluded that technological civilization has become dehumanizing.

Although as an engineer I am hardly an unbiased observer, I would like to say I find it harder to conceive of a more mischievous and poisonous set of conclusions. The fact of the matter is that ours is a technological civilization, and that tens of millions of Americans would be living in poverty, disease, and ignorance if it were not. It is time that the case was put loudly and repeatedly in the public forums that the engineering sciences are as humanizing and civilizing a human endeavor as art, philosophy, medicine, law, or music. Engineers do not have to apologize to anyone in this regard, and it is time they quit being bashful about their accomplishments.

A recent study by the world health organization found that 80 percent—80 percent—of all the world's sickness and disease is attributable to contaminated water. Those who sneer at 'technological fixes', might ponder that statistic, together with the number of persons involved - - 400 million cases a year of gastroenteritis, 250 million of elephantiasis, 160 million of malaria, 30 million of river blindness. If these afflictions seem far away, one need only visit the cemeteries of any of dozens of Colorado mountain towns to realize how many American children were claimed by typhoid and dysentery before the engineering profession made pure drinking water and efficient sewage disposal something we take for granted.

By the same token, those who speak of the need for better communication between people as a means of improving relations must either affirm the contribution of technology or stand indicted for hypocrisy. Our communications system is almost entirely a function of high technology, whether it manifests itself as a television signal sent by satellite around the globe, a phone call direct-dialed across the country, or merely in a humble postcard carried across the continent by jumbo jet.

While one can hardly deny that engineering has been abused and misused all too often, the fact it can be turned to ill ends is hardly a reason for abandoning its pursuit, any more than the existence of less-than-admirable politicians and attorneys is a reason for abandoning political science or the law.

The provision of abundant low-cost energy in the past is not just a contribution to our physical well being; it has been a principal factor behind the economic growth which has sustained the extension of our democratic institutions. The success or failure of the engineering profession in solving the energy crisis may well determine the continued well being of democracy. The fact of the matter is that beggars fighting over a crust of bread don't pay much attention to the legal niceties, fair play, or dissent.

What all this suggests is that the next few years will hold no shortage of challenges for either the engineering profession or engineering education.

The most immediate challenge, I would maintain, is not technical, but political, in the broadest sense of the term. It is the need to restore public confidence in the ability of the human intellect to solve human problems. So I would like to conclude on a note pitched directly at you. You—like lawyers, and doctors, and dentists—can be the most effective advocates for your profession. Unlike other professionals, however, engineers have tended to avoid the advocacy role. I would suggest that neither the engineering profession nor the country at large can afford to have that silence continue. Is it worth speaking up for engineers? You better believe it, and do something about it.

The Rocky Mountain Writers Guild
Annual Banquet, May 10, 1975
Denver, CO

IN THE BEGINNING WAS THE WORD

My friend Jim Hutchinson honored me with the invitation to be a guest at your annual festivity, and I want to acknowledge the pleasure of your company with a word of appreciation for the objectives of your organization and all the encouragement I can give you in pursuit of perfecting your craft.

I come from a family which was devoted to a book—the unique religious and literary classic of our Judeo-Christian culture. My father was a Lutheran minister. I learned early from that book that "In the beginning was the Word." Language has been one of the essential skills making possible the evolution of man and the aggrandizement of his arts and sciences. Writing remains the most effective transmitter and enduring form of language. Writing that achieves its proper purposes is of inestimable social value. I applaud your interest in writing and your banding together to share the aspirations of the craft and to improve your skill.

Our common language is English. It is not spoken or read by a majority of the inhabitants of the planet, and I make no chauvinistic plea for its preeminence or extension. It is a fact, however, that English has acquired the richest vocabulary and connotations and that it is now the nearest thing to a common language for science, technology, and international discourse. It has attained this status for other reasons also but in large part by a gargantuan capacity for absorbing words from other languages and coining new ones and by a cheerful indifference to the restrictions of linguistic logic. Because the rules for spelling, pronunciation, and grammar have so many exceptions, it is not only a very difficult second language to master but is probably the most misused native language in the world.

So there is much to delight in and despair of in this language of ours. And learning to love it and learning to use it correctly are an education and an art beyond the lifetime of anyone. But much can be taught and a great deal learned in a lifetime without quibbling over the hypothetical question whether Shakespeare would have profited from belonging to an Elizabethan writers guild. Some good writing in English, to be sure, is still being done. The evidence of bad writing is overwhelming. Anyone in a university, for example, who is concerned with the "common decencies" of composition—to use the phrase of the long-time head of the ontime Department of English in Engineering at CU, the late Otto Birk—can tell you that. Too much writing, even sometimes at the Ph.D. dissertation level, employs phonetic spelling and otherwise exhibits ineptitudes in word usage and in organization, construction and logic.

And if merely adequate writing of English is hardly overabundant, truly professional writing is definitely in short supply. I said professional writing rather than professional writers deliberately. I am not qualified to advise you on what the potential market is for people who would like to make writing, creative or otherwise, their career. I do have some qualifications for commenting on professional writing, I like to think, as a former engineering teacher who has published and as a university administrator with more writing obligations than I can possibly meet and with a great deal of writing to approve. And in my current assignment especially, the volume of material which stacks up on my desk is appalling. In what the Germans call the Papierkrieg, I fight at best a holding action.

I want to tick off a few concerns as the kind of reader whom you may want to keep in mind as you strive to make your writing more professional. For regardless how you start or end up earning your primary livelihood, there are so many careers and so many other ways to serve in your communities, in which the ability to write well can be a vital asset.

One of my exasperations is that most of the stuff that reaches my desk takes much too long to make the points I should not ignore. Maybe you've already heard the story of the little girl and the book about the penguins. When she took the volume back to the library, the librarian asked her how she liked it. And the little girl solemnly replied: "Well, it was all right, but it told me a lot more about penguins than I really wanted to know." I suggest that you always put yourself in the place of the reader you want to reach and err on the side of telling him less than you may think he ought to want to know. Further, take more time to be terse. It's amazing how much fat can be boiled out of most writing without the loss of anything but flabbiness. A lean style leaps, has more punch.

Another gripe of mine as a reader is the specialized vocabulary. The jargon of my colleagues in engineering; the cliches of my fellow educational administrators; the gobbledygook of bureaucrats; the double-talk of politicians; the rhetoric of right, left, and middle in just about every controversial issue—they all make my gorge rise. The more so because I am only too well aware of the temptation to resort to the same sort of thing myself. Fight it. Try hard to write exactly what you mean for the kind of reader you yourself would like to be treated as: the intelligent layman who doesn't want to be cowed, tricked, confused, cajoled, or addressed like a social security number, but just wants the facts and the real message.

A third complaint I have as a reader is pretty closely related to the second. Martin Luther may have had his difficulties trying to explicate the more esoteric refinements of Christian theology, but when he wrote about a spade, he called it a spade. I always liked that about his style. The tendency people have to exploit the language for status purposes is amusing, but now and then it bugs me. One way this is done is by displacing words that are feared to have unpleasant connotations by other words considered more agreeable or antiseptic.

There's a classic example in engineering. We used to teach a course called water supply and sewerage. Sewerage is a straightforward, explicit term. But, alas, it had to be deodorized to sanitary engineering. Another change is likely if sanitary stops smelling like a rose with another name. Conversely, other words suddenly rise in the social scale and get over-appropriated. I don't mean to be unkind or unfair, but isn't it interesting that my good old department of civil engineering is now the department of civil and environmental engineering and that the School of Architecture has now blossomed into the College of Environmental Design? May I urge you to resist this proclivity in either direction in your writing, for the good of the language and the depollution of conscious snobbery.

Let me conclude with a restatement of the basic proposition I'm trying to make about the writing I'm most familiar with from my differing perspectives of the engineering faculty and of general administration. From the administrative viewpoint I see the academic focus as losing sight of the forest for the trees. Every little discipline, with pressure applied from its journal and textbook editors, seems hell bent on developing a unique vocabulary, indeed its own grammar and style book, so that only persons admitted to the brotherhood can understand the language.

At the same time, the kowtowing to the ideals of scientific objectivity and scholarly impersonality in the professional schools, the social sciences, and even the humanities has dehumanized writing. It has drained it of color, warmth, humor, and an occasional dash of flamboyance, of every element conceding that, after all, the writer and his readers are human beings. It's as if the Nobel Prize for literature ought to be awarded to a computer.

All right, I'm exaggerating. But, quite earnestly, I urge you to strive to become common writers for common readers. The splendor of the Bible and Shakespeare's works, entirely aside from the inexhaustible veins of ore they provide the scholars, lies in the enduring universality of their appeal. This is not because they are written down to aim at some mythical level of intelligence such as the twelve-year-old's. Shakespeare's vocabulary has enormous range and some of his terms and idioms are already archaic. Our still favorite translation of the Bible is not in either basic or contemporary English. These masterpieces survive, because they still reach the minds and hearts of nearly everyone who hears or reads them.

Best wishes in your endeavors. Yours is an indispensable craft. In the beginning was the Word, and in the perpetuation of its proper use man hopefully will continue his ascent.

National Association of Accountants
Annual Convention, March 15, 1978
The Regency Inn, Denver, CO

Thank you. It is a pleasure to be with you this evening.

Of the many different publics I have the privilege to meet with as President of the University of Colorado, I think the times I value most are those occasions when I can break bread with groups of professionals such as yourselves. You're the people who practice what we at the University preach—be it medicine, law, engineering, or accounting, or any of a number of other professions—and I am delighted to be able to get out among you.

It is also reassuring to see so many of our alumni here, if for no other reason than it suggests you're gainfully employed, and this is the time of year when members of the legislature are apt to ask all those pointed questions about whether or not we are doing anything practical on the campus. Seriously, I am particularly happy to have the opportunity to be with you tonight and to renew the acquaintance with so many old friends.

This evening I would like to share with you some thoughts I've had on a topic which isn't very popular anymore. I would like to talk to you about progress.

Progress used to be one of our favorite subjects as Americans. In fact, if there was anything we were agreed on, it was the inevitability of progress and its desirability.

That doesn't seem to be the case anymore. While once our instinct was to see the promise in innovation, today we seem to dwell on the peril. Where once we emphasized the benefits of new technologies, of new ways of doing things, lately we seem to be obsessed with the costs.

I think most of us recognize the many reasons why this is so.

Public repugnance with the Asian war engendered a deep suspicion of the technology with which it was fought.

The environmental movement focused public attention on some real and serious abuses that had occurred in the course of the swift industrialization.

The creation of larger and larger urban areas, together with the deterioration of vital services in almost every major American city, caused many Americans to question both whether bigger was better and whether the technologies which made the megalopolis possible were really a constructive force.

Perhaps most significantly, the advent of the energy crisis has shaken national confidence both in the technologies which led to our overdependence on non-replenishable resources and in the ability of science and industry to solve our problems.

In a very real sense, the proponents of progress triggered a revolution of rising expectations. When those expectations exceeded the ability of science and industry to meet them, an overreaction in the other direction occurred. People began to wonder if science and industry could do anything right.

Tonight I would like to submit to you the proposition that indeed they can. I would argue that not only can science and industry solve most of the major problems facing us if given the chance to do so, but that if they are not permitted to, our future as a civilization is in real jeopardy. Moreover, I would maintain that the solutions are much closer to accrualization than is commonly realized. In the last few years, American colleges and universities have not received anywhere near the public attention that they did in the 1960s, largely because the ferment that shook the campuses then has receded.

While I should hasten to assure you that those of us in university administration are thankful for the blessed tranquility of today, it would be a major error to conclude that there has been any serious dilution of intellectual activity. In a very real sense, the turmoil of the 1960s simply moved from the administration building to the laboratory. The result has been a series of discoveries that are about to revolutionize almost every aspect of our lives.

Let me offer two examples from just two fields, biology and electronics.

About three years ago, Professor Keith Porter of our faculty removed the nucleus from a living cell and transplanted it into another cell. The transplant took; that is to say the recipient cell began displaying the characteristics of the donor and transmitted them to its daughter cell.

The technique has since been widely adopted by molecular biologists and is a major tool both use in their work. In just three years that work bounded far beyond Professor Porter's accomplishment. Today molecular biology is systematically unraveling the double helix and in detail describing structure and the mechanisms by which the various genes control the functions of life.

Such a theory would make possible the rational design and synthesis of drugs to treat specific maladies. If that doesn't appear to be a major accomplishment, remember that even today most drugs are discovered by trial and error testing. In this regard, medicine is not nearly as far removed from Pasteur, as we would like to think it is.

Now, however, we can expect that before long, biologists who cannot "find" a cure for a disease will design one. Perhaps someone will synthesize a cure for the common cold. Indeed, about a year ago it was announced that the first anti-viral agent was undergoing specific tests.

Other workers in the field are altering the genes in various organisms, in effect creating new species. So far, attention has focused on the dangers of research in DNA, as this work is called. I would like to point to some of the possibilities. Creation of a yeast that converted sugar to alcohol more efficiently could ultimately have more impact on the energy crisis than the development of the breeder reactor.

The accomplishments in biology are being matched by those in electronics. This is one area where it is hardly necessary to belabor the point, because the products of the semi-conductor revolution are already arriving in the marketplace. I'm certain most of you are already familiar with the enormous amount of computing power that is now available to even the smallest corporation. There is no doubt in my mind that within 10 years, each of you will have in your offices—possibly in your briefcases—a computer with as much power as the one that just ten years ago the University of Colorado paid $3 million for. Ours, of course, occupies half the basement of a major building, and required the constant ministrations of several dozen programmers and their acolytes.

The managerial revolution this should bring about is staggering to contemplate. I suspect the prospect of accounting in real time is the least of it. The availability of such tools will make it possible to do things never before contemplated. I suspect that most people consider professions such as accounting and university governance staid, mature callings that have not greatly changed since the development of double entry and boards of trustees. Ah, if they only knew.

Semi-conductors, of course, are finding applications far beyond business machines. Computers on a chip are being used for everything from monitoring and controlling the family car to guiding artillery shells. The semi-conductor industry is the one area of the economy that has seen both absolute declines in product costs on an on-going basis during an unprecedented period of inflation. Those products, which can incorporate these components, obviously share in those savings. Those industries that emulate the semi-conductor industry—those which in the words of Buckminster Fuller succeed in doing more with less—are the ones which are most apt to transcend the present so-called crises.

I suspect that the real contribution of the electronics industry and the molecular biologist and many other scientists and researchers working on the cutting edges of inquiry goes far beyond the various application of their finding. However, in order to illustrate this point, let me go back in history a few hundred years.

When Europe began to discover the world in the 15th and 16th centuries the development of precise tools of navigation became critical. It was not long before navigators discovered their most pressing need was a means of measuring time precisely; in other words, they needed a clock that kept time with an accuracy approaching that of a Mickey Mouse wrist watch.

The development of such a timepiece required unprecedented advances in technology. Metals of unheard of hardness, durability, and ductility had to be developed. Components had to be fashioned to unbelievable fine tolerances. The whole science of precision engineering had to be invented from scratch. New materials, new techniques, new processes, and new ways of solving problems all had to be developed.

The world's first accurate clocks were, of course, revolutionary in their own right. Not only did they make accurate navigation possible, but also they gave western civilization an unprecedented sense of time. It can be argued that they touched off a managerial revolution as profound and far-reaching as anything the computer can do in our time.

But just as profound was the revolution set off by the technology developed in making the clocks. Because of that technology, the precision tooling, the materials fabricating, and the design techniques laid the foundation for the industrial revolution.

I suspect the same thing may be happening today. The technology that permits the semi-conductor industry to put 500,000 transistors on a single chip of silicon may be more important than the chip itself. The technique that permits the molecular biologist to detect the presence of a single atom may be more important than anything he does with it.

History teaches us, I think, that when technology lets a genie out of a bottle the most profound results are almost never mentioned in our first three wishes.

The point I'm trying to make, I guess, is that the day of science and technology is far from done. There are plenty of dances in the old girl yet. And the reason I'm even troubling you with these somewhat disconnected ramblings is a serious one. We used to say that you can't stand in the way of progress. But recently people have discovered you can.

I submit that as a civilization there is no single more dangerous thing that we can do. The fact of the matter is that we are a technical civilization and we cannot find salvation by trying to deny our roots. That, of course, holds only stagnation, decay, and ruin.

The great fact of American life has been the ability of American science and industry to maintain an economy that was able to keep offering more and more people an ever-widening variety of choices. One consequence of our two centuries of economic growth has been to establish a continually rising level of expectations among our people. Until very recently, expectations—and our ability to meet them—have to a large extent determined the ethos of American civilization.

Historically, our economy has been sustained by abundant supplies of energy and materials. The advent of the energy crisis, however, raises a real question as to our continued ability to obtain the quantities of energy necessary to sustain economic expansion at a pace sufficient to meet our national expectations. The failure to do so is then a blow to our national self confidence. It goes to the very heart of the continued well being of our social fabric.

To put it bluntly, beggars fighting over a slice of bread don't have much respect for the democratic process and the legal niceties.

It is by no means obvious, or even likely, that we will ultimately fail to solve our energy problems and return to a course of sustained economic growth and increases in productivity. But it is absolutely certain that success depends on our willingness to affirm our commitment to science, technology, and the ability of the human intellect to fashion solutions to human problems—to what in a more genteel age used to be called progress.

I do not mean to minimize the risks and abuses associated with progress. To do so would be to ignore some very important lessons of the past 30 years.

Nevertheless, I think it is time to reemphasize the promise of innovation and not dwell exclusively on the peril. As the president of a university engaged in extensive research, I admit to being biased in this regard, but I submit that bias comes in part from seeing the possibilities of what that research can accomplish if given a chance.

Perhaps the late Robert Kennedy put it best when he said, "Some men see the world as it is and ask why. But I see things that never were and ask why not."

Rautenstraus' Farewell Address (as CU president)
The Summer Commencement, August 18, 1979
The quadrangle in front of Old Main, Boulder, CO

I would like to share with you a few thoughts about the fundamental purposes of the University. I think that is an appropriate thing to do inasmuch as many of us will be leaving it, and leave-takings lead one to reflect on concluded affairs.

Obviously one fundamental purpose of the institution has to do with why you are here today, that is to offer you instruction and to provide you with the opportunity to educate yourselves in the years ahead.

I hardly have to lecture you on how important and valuable that function of the University is. Most of you have invested four years of your time and some $15,000 to $20,000 in your educations, and you are to be congratulated on what you have accomplished.

Given that sort of an investment, you have every right to expect the best education the University and its faculty is capable of offering, and that points to the second, and more fundamental, purpose of the University.

That purpose is, simply stated, to conduct a relentless and uncompromising search for the truth.

We undertake that search for several reasons. One is because to do any less would mean that you would be receiving an inferior education. Your degrees would be worth very little if they represented a perfect knowledge of inaccurate information.

Another reason we undertake that search is that society expects us to. Our civilization has learned through hard historic experience that its continued economic, intellectual, and social vigor depends upon the existence of places where unfettered individuals have the charge to seek the truth, no matter where the trail leads.

But if most people are prepared to subscribe to these notions in the abstract, they are not nearly as popular when it comes to specifics. The fact of the matter is that there is no shortage of special lobbies who would prefer the institution to be warped in a manner that reflects their particular point of view.

The most obvious of these are those that make a frontal attack, demanding that ideas they find odious be suppressed, and attempting to force feed their own concepts and beliefs into the mainstream of the institution's intellectual life.

But if such attacks are the most extravagant, they are also the easiest to repel, by virtue of their being essentially alien to the fundamental values of the Republic. The more successful attacks are those which are more subtle.

They are the ones which may originate with elected and appointed officials who under the cover of broad oversight and budgetary authority promulgate rules, limitations, and regulations for the purpose of controlling the life of the institution in its most minute specifics. For example, individuals who themselves would find the notion of burning books to be offensive have no difficulty at all, either with their consciences or their constituencies, in cutting, earmarking, and otherwise manipulating library budgets.

Nor are attempts to warp the institution to fit a particular point of view confined to those outside the academic community. The process can be initiated by administrators who govern in an atmosphere of fear and retribution, imposing an excessive conformity out of administrative convenience. It can be initiated by faculty, who through tenure decisions, creation of departments, and control of curriculum can exclude whole areas of inquiry from the institution while promoting others. It can be initiated by students, who through demands for relevancy, may consciously or unconsciously restrict discussion and study of unpopular or controversial points of view.

And, if you will allow me one last admonition, the process can be initiated by alumni, who propose to preserve the institution unchanged and unchanging as they knew it during the period in which they were enrolled.

Well, regardless of the source or motivation, such attempts to warp the institution to a particular view must be combated. Above all other things, universities have a responsibility for the defense of tolerance, not because scholars are the chosen few, but because tolerance is absolutely essential for any meaningful inquiry.

During his days as American ambassador to the United Nations, Sen. Daniel Patrick Moynahan was fond of saying he wanted us to be feared for the truth we would tell. Even if there is a tragic dimension to that vision, it is nevertheless an infinitely more desirable fate than being feared because you act out of self-induced ignorance.

The point I am trying to make is the academy can give away almost everything and still survive. The exception is the right of those who are here to search for truth and to speak it. When that is given away, the academy becomes an elegant, empty shell, devoid of any real meaning, substance, or significance. And when that happens, not just the university, but mankind itself is the loser.

It has been a pleasure to have you at the University. I hope that you will always find it worthwhile to return.

PRESIDENTS OF THE
UNIVERSITY OF COLORADO

1877-1887	Joseph A. Sewall
1887-1892	Horace M. Hale
1892-1914	James H. Baker
1914-1919	Livingston Farrand
1919-1939	George Norlin
1939-1953	Robert L. Stearns
1953-1956	Ward Darley
1956-1963	Quigg Newton
1963-1969	Joseph R. Smiley
1969 (June-Sept.)	Eugene Wilson
1969-1974	Frederick P. Thieme
1974-1980	**Roland C. Rautenstraus***
1980-1985	Arnold Weber
1985-1986	William Baughn
1986-1990	Gordon Gee
1990-1991	William Baughn
1991-1996	Judith Albino
1996- —	John Buechner

* From April 1974 until December 1974 Rautenstraus was interim president.

REGENTS

(during Rautenstraus' tenure as president and executive vice president)

1972-1984	Jack Kent Anderson*
1962-1974	Dale M. Atkins
1972-1978	Geraldine Bean*
1975-1980	Louis F. Bein*
1976-1982	Fred Betz, Jr.*
	(also, 1956-62)
1964-1976	Fred Betz, Sr.
1975-1980	Richard J. Bernick*
	(also, 1958-60, 1960-66)
1966-1972	Harry G. Carlson
1975-1976	Jim R. Carrigan
1966-1972	Joseph Coors
1979-1996	Peter Dietze*
1968-1974	Robert M. Gilbert
1970-1982	Byron L. Johnson*
1976-1982	Sandy Kraemer*
1964-1970	Daniel F. Lynch
1973-1976	Thomas S. Moon
1973-1974	Raphael J. Moses
1976-1984	Rachel Noel*
1972-1978	Eric W. Schmidt*
1979-1989	David Sunderland*

Indicates regents during the Rautenstraus presidency.

223

DEANS
(College of Engineering and Applied Science)**

1893-1902	Henry Fulton
1902-1903	George H. Rowe
1903-1905	Henry B. Dates
1905-1919	Milo S. Ketchum
1919-1943	Herbert S. Evans
1943-1960	Clarence L. Eckel
1960-1962	Charles A. Hutchinson (acting dean)
1962-1978	Max S. Peters
1978-1980	William Pietenpol
1980-1981	Frank Barnes (interim dean)
1981-1994	A. Richard Seebass
1994- —	Ross Corotis

**Note: Established as the School of Applied Science. Changed to the College of Engineering in 1906, then changed to the College of Engineering and Applied Science.

CHAIRS
(Department of Civil, Architectural and Environmental Engineering)***

1893-1901	Henry Fulton
1901-1904	Charles Derleth, Lindsay Duncan
1904-1919	Milo S. Ketchum
1919-1926	W. C. Huntington
1926-1943	Clarence L. Eckel
1943-1959	Warren Raeder
1959-1964	**Roland C. Rautenstraus**
1964 (June-July)	Leo Novak (acting chair)
1964-1972	Robert S. Ayre
1972-1976	Leonard G. Tulin
1976-1977	J. Ernest Flack (acting chair)
1977-1983	George G. Goble
1983-1990	Hon-Yim Ko
1990-1991	Stein Sture
1991-1994	James P. Heaney
1994-1998	Stein Sture
1998- —	Hon-Yim Ko

***Note: Originally named the Department of Civil Engineering, then the Department of Civil and Architectural Engineering (1962), it was re-named the Department of Civil, Architectural and Environmental Engineering in 1970.

(Department of Architectural Engineering)****

1926-1943	Clarence L. Eckel
1943-1952	Warren Raeder
1952-1959	Thomas L Hansen
1959-1962	DeVon M. Carlson (acting chair)
1962	Robert E. Rathburn (coordinator)

****Note: In 1962, the School of Architecture was established with DeVon Carlson as dean. The operation of architectural engineering then merged into the Department of Civil Engineering and, in 1970, that department expanded and added environmental engineering: The Department of Civil, Architectural and Environmental Engineering was the resulting name.

225

SOURCE MATERIALS

SELECT BOOKS & NEWSPAPER ARTICLES

Allen, F. S., Andrade, E., Jr., Foster, M. S., Mitterling, P. I. and Scamehorn, H. L., *The University of Colorado 1876-1976*. Harcourt Brace Jovanovich, Inc., New York, 1976

Athearn, R., *High Country Empire*. University of Nebraska Press, Lincoln, NE, 1965

Armstrong, M., "Berry denies she would serve in HEW post 4-8 years," *Colorado Daily*, March 28, 1977

Blake, P., "Embattled CU chief fights back — hard," *Rocky Mountain News*, October 18, 1970

Blocker, K., "Ex-president sees a more conservative CU," *Colorado Daily*, January 11-13, 1991

Branscombe, A., "Colorado Approaching Crossroads, Retiring C.U. President Says," *The Denver Post*, January 13, 1980

Branscombe, A., "CU Needs President? Yes — Rautenstraus," *The Denver Post*, September 1979

Branscombe, A., "Heading CU 'Constraining'," *The Denver Post*, March 11, 1979

Branscombe, A., "'Money' Key Word in CU President's List of Top 4 Needs," *The Denver Post*, September 24, 1978

Brady, D., "President Defends Action," *The Washington Post*, December 21, 1978

Butman, B., "Memorial March Honors Dead Chicanos," *Daily Camera*, July 5, 1974

Cain, D., "Former CU president returns to teaching," *CU Campus Press*, November 17, 1988

Carroll, J., "Rautenstraus reminisces on former CU presidency," *CU Campus Press*, November 19, 1981

Casotti, F., *The Golden Buffaloes: Colorado Football*. Strode Publishers, Huntsville, AL, 1980

Castrone, L., "CU Holds Off on Salary Challenge," *Daily Camera*, Boulder, July 20, 1979

Castrone, L., "Lancredo Answers Regents on CU Chief," *Daily Camera*, July 31, 1979

Castrone, L., "CU's Rautenstraus Ready to Be Replaced," *Sunday Camera*, Boulder, September 30, 1979

Chen, F.H., and Weingardt, R., *Engineering Colorado*. Jacqueline-Palamar Publishing, Denver, 1989

Cornett, L., "CU Class of 1946 Plans Reunion: Ex-classmates Fondly Recall WW II Days," *The Denver Post*, April 21, 1996

Cornett, L., "CU Regents Unanimously Okay First Black Female Chancellor," *Daily Camera*, Boulder, CO, January 23, 1976

Cornett, L., "Rautenstraus Selected CU President," *Daily Camera*, January 14, 1975

Cornett, L., "Regents Enthusiastic Over Rautenstraus," *Daily Camera*, January 15, 1975

Cornett, L., "Thieme Fired By CU Regents," *Daily Camera*, April 25, 1974

Cosper, D., "Deadly '70s Activism," *Daily Camera*, May 4, 1994

Cracraft, J., "He Loves Being Up Creek," *The Denver Post*, September 1976

Curtis, O., "'Glory, Glory Colorado:' Does Big = Great?," *Sunday Empire, The Denver Post*, Vol. 19, No. 18

Curtin, D., "Ex-CU Chief Rautenstraus Dies," *The Denver Post*, December 27, 1997

Davis, W. E., *Glory Colorado!: A History of the University of Colorado 1858-1963*. Pruett Press, Inc., Boulder, 1965

Deans, S., "Marchers Remember Deaths of 'Los Seis de Boulder',"
Sunday Camera, May 28, 1978

Deans, S., "Rally Draws 3,000 CU Backers," *Daily Camera*, March 8,
1979

Deans, S., "'Weary' Rautenstraus Resigns CU Post," *Daily Camera*,
March 7, 1979

Dedmon, J., "Mary Berry resigns as chancellor at CU," *Rocky Mountain News*, May 1977.

Dillard, S., "Living Standards Tied to Education," *The Denver Post*,
August 1976

Domash, L., "Rautenstraus: I'm a captive of the people," *Colorado Daily*, February 6, 1976

Ellis, R., and Smith, D., *Colorado: A History in Photographs*. University Press of Colorado, Niwot, CO, 1991

Guffey, S. J., "70s a Decade of Drastic Change, Tragedy for Colorado," *The Denver Post*, January 1, 1980

Haraway, F., "New CU Arena To Seat 13,000," *The Denver Post*, August 13, 1969

Helstrom, J., "Regent Vote Bars SDS From University Status," *Daily Camera*, November 23, 1968

Helstrom, J., "SDS Meeting Approved," *Daily Camera*, September 21, 1968

Hilliard, C., "Governor Praises Rautenstraus," *Daily Camera*, March 8, 1979

James, R., *Our Own Generation*. University of Colorado, Boulder, 1979

Johnson, J., "Fall Opening Is Scheduled," *The Free Press*, Colorado Springs, August 7, 1965

Jordon, B., "Temporary Injunction Denied in Grand Jury Bombing Probe," *Daily Camera*, July 11, 1974

Leach, J., "CU President's Cadillac Donated By Local Dealer," *Daily Camera*, October 8, 1977

Lindstrom, C., "CU to Merge Men's, Women's Athletics," *Daily Camera*, April 27, 1978

Little, W. T., "Sanatorium, 80-Acre Plot Donated to CU in Springs," *Rocky Mountain News*, October, 1964

McGraw, P., "Rautenstraus Evaluates Self, CU Role in Light of New Post," *The Denver Post*, January 19, 1975

McGraw, P., "Regents Ask Record Budget of $162 Million for 1977-78," *The Denver Post*, August 20, 1976

McGraw, P. "Regents Fire CU's Thieme," *The Denver Post*, April 25, 1974

McGraw, P., "Thieme Rumored to Resign Soon," *The Denver Post*, April 12, 1974

Merkowitz, D., "Interview With President Rautenstraus, *Silver &Gold Record*, January 28, 1975

Moss, I., "AFA-CU Series Finale Is Just Another Game," *The Denver Post*, September 3, 1974

Muilenburg, G. and Swineford, A., *Land of the Post Rock*. University Press of Kansas, Lawrence, 1976

Murray, J. E., "CU President Views Sports, Academics, Frogs," *Daily Camera*, January 9, 1977

Norgaard, W., "Rautenstraus: Teacher from start to finish," *Colorado Daily*, November 5, 1985

Nuchum, M. B., "CU's interim president a creature of the University," *Rocky Mountain News*, June 30, 1974

Paddock, L., "Rautenstraus: Know Value as Well as Price," *Daily Camera*, October 15, 1979

Paddock, L., "Rautenstraus Stripped of Title as Youngest CU President," *Daily Camera*, September 8, 1978

Peltz, J., "CU research stands strong amidst emphasis on teaching," *Colorado Daily*, December 13, 1977

Penfold, P., "Raut reflects on 50 years at CU," *Colorado Alumnus*, September 1996

Rautenstraus, R., "Africa Goes To School," *Aurora Borealis* (*Silver &Gold Record* monthly supplement), December 13, 1977

Rautenstraus, R., "Inflation (Everybody talks about it, but nobody does anything about it)," *Rocky Mountain News*, October 4, 1979

Rautenstraus, R., "Potholes, not Iran, are America's crisis," *Rocky Mountain News*, May 15, 1980

Rautenstraus, R., "Research at Educational Institutions," *Vital Speeches Of The Day*, Vol. XLV, No. 17, June 15, 1979

Rees, T., "Rautenstraus: CU founding is 1st priority," *Rocky Mountain News*, January 19, 1975

Rees, T., "Thieme is dismissed as president of CU," *Rocky Mountain News*, April 27, 1974

Sealing, K., "Raut: economy University's biggest foe," *Colorado Daily*, January 20, 1975

Sealing, K., "Choosing new CU president may take a while," *Colorado Daily*, June 13, 1974

Sheeler, J., "His Blood Cells Would Have CU on Them," *Boulder Planet*, February 11-17, 1998

Shipley, M. and Siegfried, M., *Proud Past...Bright Future*. University of Colorado/College of Engineering, Boulder, 1966

Shribman, D., "Small Town, Big Dream," *The Boston Globe*, March 17, 1995

Shribman, D., "The Making of Bob Dole," *The Boston Globe*, June 18, 1995

Sonn, B., "Rautenstraus: The Making of The President," *The Straight Creek Journal*, January 21, 1975

Stoenner, A., "Rautenstraus expects CU urban programs to be in Denver," *Fourth Estate*, Denver, February 5, 1975

Tuchman, J., "Administrator: times change, but not that much," (Interview of R. Rautenstraus), *Colorado Daily*, August 7, 1973

Waidmann, B., "Rautenstraus: 30 years of loyalty at CU," *Colorado Daily*, May 2, 1974

Weiss, S., and Gorishek, W., "Eastern provost to head CU," *Rocky Mountain News*, November 2, 1979

White, N., "Former CU President 'Raut' Dies," *Daily Camera*, Boulder, CO, December 27, 1997

Wiscombe, J., "'Raut' Enjoys His New Role," *Daily Camera*, Boulder, CO, August 31, 1981

————— "A 'startling' proposal: How CU can be saved from Legislature," *Rocky Mountain News*, October 28, 1979

————— "Centennial Medalists," *CUEngineering*, No. 11, 1994

————— "Chicano students briefly take over office at CU," *Rocky Mountain News*, October 31, 1973

————— "Colleges: 'Most Serious Crisis Since Civil War,'" *Fort Morgan Times*, May 8, 1970

————— "CU Freshman To Reap Benefits of 'ZPG'," *Town and Country Review*, August 4, 1974

————— "Dean of Men, Women Titles Abolished; Titles, Scope of Duties Broadened," *Daily Camera*, August 17, 1968

————— "Executive V.P., University Relations," *Coloradan*, Vol. 76, pp. 86-88, 1974

————— "Five Alumni To Be Honored At CU Engineering Fete," *Daily Camera*, Boulder, April 3, 1975

————— "Former C.U. President Honored for Contributions to Engineering," *ACEC/CO Newsletter*, Vol. 6, Issue 3, March 1996

————— "Judge Blocks Colo. Hiring of Fairbanks: Colorado Loses in U.S. Court," *The Washington Post*, January 16, 1979

————— "'Leave' surprises CU's Rautenstraus," *Rocky Mountain News*, March 28, 1977

————— "Nine UNC alumni to be honored Nov. 1," *Greeley Tribune*, Colorado, October 18, 1975

————— "Profiles: Roland C. Rautenstraus," *Daily Camera*, September 1977

————— "Rautenstraus: An administrator for the students," *CU Perspective*, October 18, 1968

————— "Rautenstraus Students' Choice For CU President," *Daily Camera*, Boulder, December 19, 1974

————— "Roland C. Rautenstraus (a poem)," *Colorado Daily*, December 18, 1979

————— "Roland Rautenstraus," *Boulder Monthly*, September 1979

————— "Roland Rautenstraus, Acting President," *Coloradan*, Vol. 77, pp. 34-35, February 1975

———— "Roland C. Rautenstraus, President of CU from 1974 to 1980," *The Denver Rocky Mountain News*, December 27, 1997

———— "Thieme Is Ousted, 7-2; Rautenstraus Named," *Silver & Gold Record*, April 26, 1974

———— "University Relations V.P. Rautenstraus Named Executive Vice President of CU," *Silver & Gold Record*, April 1973

———— "University Report: Roland Rautenstraus Profile," *Daily Camera*, March 7, 1985

———— "UNM Will Honor Two," *Albuquerque Journal*, April 29, 1976

———————————————

SELECT CORRESPONDENCE

February 20, 1940 letter from the Governor of Kansas

June 3, 1941 letter from the Wheat Ridge Superintendent of Schools

July 1, 1941 letter from University of Denver, Department of Athletics

October 1, 1946 letter from President's Office, University of Colorado

May 20, 1947 letter from American Society of Civil Engineers

July 8, 1947 letter from President's Office, University of Colorado

June 14, 1954 letter from President's Office, University of Colorado

December 21, 1954 letter from City of Boulder, Colorado

February 3, 1958 letter from City of Boulder, Colorado

July 8, 1967 letter from President's Office, University of Colorado

August 15, 1967 letter from John A. Love, governor of Colorado

February 20, 1959 letter from President's Office, University of Colorado

December 2, 1968 letter from Richard M. Nixon, president-elect

May 24, 1973 letter from Colorado Governor John Love

June 13, 1973 letter from Wendell Burchett, chair CU staff
    council

March 15, 1976 letter from President's Office, University of New
    Mexico

December 6, 1977 letter from Bill Mallory (CU) to Robert Six

December 20, 1977 letter from Robert Six to Bill Mallory (CU)

December 28, 1977 letter from Robert Six, Continental Airlines

September 26, 1978 letter from Robert Six, Continental Airlines

October 2, 1978 letter from Ira Rothgerber, Rothgerber, Appel &
    Powers

October 11, 1978 letter from Roland Rautenstraus to Robert F. Six

October 20, 1978 letter from Robert Six, Continental Airlines

December 14, 1979 letter from Board of Regents, University of
    Colorado

MISCELLANEOUS

Archives: University of Colorado at Boulder Libraries (Presidential
    papers, and files of Rautenstraus when vice president and ex-
    ecutive vice president)

Church archives of Evangelical Lutheran Church of America,
    Chicago

Church records of: Emmanuel Lutheran, Hoisington, KS; St. John's
    Lutheran, Russell, KS; St. Peter's Lutheran, Creston, NE and
    Zion Lutheran, Gothenburg, NE

Collection of Rautenstraus speeches: 1974 to 1979 (Archives of the
    College of Engineering, University of Colorado at Boulder)

Interview of Roland Rautenstraus by Pam Penfold, 1996 (uncut and
    unedited), Boulder, CO

Memorial Service Account: Reported in *Silver & Gold Record*, Boulder,
    CO, February 12, 1998

Norlin Award Nomination (of Rautenstraus) Packet by Eugene Wilson, February 14, 1974

Obituaries from *The Denver Post* and *Rocky Mountain News*: Ruth Dumler (April 15, 1982), Christian R. (Nov. 27, 1979), Emma R. (July 20, 1964), Roland R. (Dec. 27, 1997) and Walter R. (Dec. 4, 1992)

Personal scrapbooks, photo albums and records of Curt Rautenstraus

Personal scrapbooks, photo albums and records of Willie Rautenstraus

Presidential papers abstracts by David Hays, Norlin Library Archives

Rautenstraus Retirement Party Slide Presentation by Laurie Paddock, 1980 (uncut and unedited), Boulder, CO

"The Life Story of Reverend Christian Rautenstraus" by Kent Rautenstraus, Wheat Ridge, CO, 1970 (An unpublished manuscript)

Video Tapes (courtesy of Sandy Hale): "Exploration of Wisdom," Channel TV 8, Boulder, CO, September 26, 1997 and "The Depression Years," Channel TV 54, Boulder, CO, June 1996. (*Rautenstraus was the main speaker on both.*)

RELEVANT INTERVIEWS

Adelstein, Robert. Denver, CO. January 8, 1999.

Adelstein, Stanford. Rapid City, SD. January 8, 1999.

Anderson, Jack Kent. Denver, CO. February 5, 1999.

Anderson, Pal. Valley Center, CA. April 2, 1999.

Banks, Edwin. Boulder, CO. February 3, 1999.

Barnes, Frank. Boulder, CO. March 11, 1999.

Bartlett, Paul. Denver, CO. January 25, 1999.

Berke, Steve. Gothenburg, NE. March 9, 1999.

Bernick, Richard. Denver, CO. February 4, 1999.

Buechner, John. Boulder, CO. January 6, 1999.

Carpenter, Ed. Grand Junction, CO. June 1, 1999.

Chamberlain, Ray. Ft. Collins, CO. March 24, 1999.

Corbridge, James. Boulder, CO. January 26, 1999.

Corotis, Lindsay. Boulder, CO. January 27, 1999.

Corotis, Ross. Boulder, CO. January 6, 1999.

Danish, Paul. Boulder, CO. January 28, 1999.

Davis, Del. Bonita Springs, FL. February 19, 1999.

Davis, Jack. Littleton, CO. March 24, 1999.

Davis, William. Baton Rouge, LA. February 26, 1999.

Dell'Apa, Edith. Boulder, CO. June 1, 1999.

Deno, William. Boulder, CO. February 10, 1999.

Dietze, Peter. Boulder, CO. March 15, 1999.

DiLorenzo, Gladys. Wheat Ridge, CO. March 27, 1999.

Downs, Shirley. Wheat Ridge, CO. April 1, 1999.

Dumler, Larry. Delta, CO. February 20, 1999.

Finley, Joe. Longmont, CO. April 1, 1999.

Fowler, David. Austin,TX. January 8, 1999.

Gallegos, Nathan. Boulder, CO. May 28, 1999.

Grimm, David. Boulder, CO. February 16, 1999.

Hale, Sandra. Boulder, CO. January 26, 1999.

Haase, Ed. Evergreen, CO. February 17, 1999.

Hays, David. Boulder, CO. January 12, 1999.

Holt, Steve. Denver, CO. January 22, 1999.

Jobman, Harvey. Gothenburg, NE. March 10, 1999.

Joselyn, JoAnn. Boulder, CO. April 16, 1999.

Kinslinger, Jack, Washington, DC. March 8, 1999.

Ko, Hon-Yim. Boulder, CO. February 16, 1999.

Koelbel, Walt. Denver, CO. February 12, 1999.

Kontny, Vince. Irvine, CA. March 3, 1999.

Lamm, Richard. Denver, CO. March 23, 1999.

Laszlo, Ted. Denver, CO. June 1, 1999.

Lisensky, Robert. Boulder, CO. April 23, 1999.

Maler, George. Boulder, CO. February 8, 1999.

Manning, Thurston. Boulder, CO. February 16, 1999.

Meheen, H. Joe. Denver, CO. February 11, 1999.

Mortenson, Mort. Minneapolis, MN. April 16, 1999.

Norman, Daniel. Denver, CO. January 22, 1999.

Nuzum, Dwayne. Boulder, CO. June 3, 1999.

Paddock, Laurie. Boulder, CO. May 25, 1999.

Penfold, Pam. Boulder, CO. March 15, 1999.

Peters, Max. Boulder, CO. February 8, 1999.

Pinchuk, Lanny. Boulder, CO. January 26, 1999.

Plank, Marj. Gothenburg, NE. March 9, 1999.

Rautenstraus, Curt. Louisville, CO. January 4, 1999.

Rautenstraus, Kent. Wheat Ridge, CO. February 4, 1999.

Rautenstraus, Willie. Boulder, CO. January 12, 1999.

Ross, Eugene. Denver, CO. February 9,1999.

Rundles, Jeff. Denver, CO. April 20, 1999.

Seebass, A. Richard. Boulder, CO. January 26, 1999.

Seeton, Frank. Lakewood, CO. March 16, 1999.

Schloss, Kristy. Denver, CO. February 2, 1999.

Siccardi, Joe. Denver, CO. February 8, 1999.

Sture, Stein. Boulder, CO. January 6, 1999.

Sturgeon, Orvene (Plank). Denver, CO. March 10, 1999.

Taylor-Schaus, Kelly. Hoisington, KS. May 1, 1999.

Tulin, Leonard. Estes Park, CO. February 11, 1999.

Weingardt, Dennis. Denver, CO. March 26, 1999.

Went, Judy. Creston, NE. March 13, 1999.

Whittman, Elisabeth. Chicago, IL. March 18, 1999.

Worthington, Carl. Boulder, CO. May 4, 1999.

Wycisk, Max. Denver, CO. April 21, 1999.

ACRONYMS

ACEC   American Consulting Engineers Council
ASCE   American Society of Civil Engineers
BSAE   Bachelor of Science, Architectural Engineering
BSBus   Bachelor of Science, Business
BSCE   Bachelor of Science, Civil Engineering
CCHE   Colorado Commission on Higher Education
CDOT   Colorado Department of Highways (Colo. Hwy. Dept.)
CE   Civil engineer, civil engineering
CPR   Colorado Public Radio
CSU   Colorado State University
CU   University of Colorado
HEW   U.S. Department of Health, education and Welfare
JBC   Joint Budget Committee (State of Colorado)
MSCE   Master of Science, Civil Engineering
NCHEMS   National Center for Higher Education Management Systems
NFL   National Football League
NSF   National Science Foundation
PCO   Photograph Courtesy of
PE   Professional Engineer (P.E.)
PLS   Professional Land Surveyor
ROTC   Reserve Officer Training Corps
SDS   Students for a Democratic Society
UCB   University of Colorado at Boulder
UCCS   University of Colorado at Colorado Springs
UCD   University of Colorado at Denver
UNC   University of Northern Colorado (Colorado State College)
UNM   University of New Mexico
WWI   World War One
WWII   World War Two

INDEX

Because Roland (Raut) Rautenstraus and the University of Colorado (CU) are mentioned extensively throughout the book, they are not listed in this Index.